Domestic Violence
and
Matrilineal Society

Christian Heritage Rediscovered

The Series, as the name suggests, is meant to focus on Christian Faith & Living vis-à-vis topics like Literature & Poetry, Indigenous Philosophizing, Ethical response towards Agriculture, Health & Healing, Science & Technology, Ecofeminist Theology, Sociological approach towards Human Rights, Law & Politics, Arts, History of Ideas, Ancient Civilizations, Cultural Contiguity, Religious Cosmologies & Mysticism, Footsteps of famous Theologians, World Peace & Harmony, Global Capitalism, Network Marketing, Cybertheology, Population & Demographics, Epigraphic Studies, Contextualized Education, and many others. We welcome a Mss. on any topic/s mentioned, whether they are original works, scholarly monographs, collections of conference papers, revised dissertations, or translations of historical documents. Through the Series we, the Publishers, are striving to put forward published works that may help Institutions, Academic Bodies, Researchers, Scholars and the World at large in furthering their respective knowledge and understanding on the concerned subject. We welcome your comments on our efforts and further suggestions on how we can foster the upcoming thoughtful theologically grounded books.

Christian Heritage Rediscovered - 81

Domestic Violence
and
Matrilineal Society

Recapturing Khasi Theological-Ethical Values

Malwin Stone Passah

CWI

Christian World Imprints

First Published in 2019 by

Christian World Imprints
Christian Publishing & Books from India
H-12 Bali Nagar, **New Delhi-110015**
info@christianworldimprints.com
www.ChristianWorldImprints.com
Phone: +91 11 25465925

ISBN: 978-93-5148-358-8 (HB)
ISBN: 978-93-5148-359-5 (PB)

Printed in India.

CONTENTS

NORTH -EASTERN HILL UNIVERSITY
SHILLONG-793022

Prof. Streamlet Dkhar
Dean, School of Humanities
NEHU, Shillong

Tel: + 91-09436117479 (M)
+ 0364 2723305 (O)
Email: s.dkhar@rediffmail.com
March 15, 2019

FOREWORD

There has been in recent years a demand of research works on different concepts of Khasi culture and matrilineal system for reference books. A number of writings that came out in the past emphasized on the lineage system and the system of inheritance practicing by the Khasis. Theoretically, the Khasis believe that women enjoy their rights and have equal status with men; this assumption has been blindly accepted not only by the outsiders but also by the Khasi people in the past years. Even many Khasi and non Khasi writers have written about the status of women to be higher as compared to our fellow counterparts practicing the patriarchal system in our neighbouring states and beyond. Many were of the view that Khasi women do not need empowerment as they are already empowered. Yet, practically the Khasis who claim to practice the matrilineal system have the only benefit that is of the lineage being traced to the mother and nothing else because all other decisions are in the hands of men. The partiarchal mindset is very much there in the Khasi society; women do face oppression and domestic violence as other women of the patriarchal society. With the research undertaken and submitted to the senate of Serampore College (University) for the Master of Theology on the topic *Domestic Violence and Matrilineal Society: Recapturing Khasi Theological-Ethical Values,* Rev. Malwin Stone Passah has made a right decision to publish this dissertation. This is a kind of reasearch which is the need of the hour to really know the matrilineal system which faces the transition today.

To briefly highlight about this book, it contains four Chapters excluding the Introduction and the Conclusion. Since the book came out of a research study, the introduction part is the research methodology that consist the statement of the problems, review of previous related literature, scope and limitation, methods and structure of research. The First chapter deals with the Khasi Society: an overview of the Khasi society in the past and the transition that takes place over the years. The chapter has been divided into a number of sections where the author has given a defininition of the term Khasi, and specifically gives an account of each of the section he has chosen: socio-cultural dimension, matrilinineal system, clan system, the family, family organisation, the role of family members, the role of mother or wife, the role of father/husband/maternal uncle, role of children, marriage, divorce, inheritance, status of men and women, economic profile, agriculture, system of land ownership, division of labour and wage policy, trade relation, political structure, the religious set up. On the traditional religious-Ethical teachings and the three basic tenets of Khasi culture: *Kamai ïa ka Hok, Tipbriew tipblei* and *tipkur tipkha*, the chapter has highlighted how these ethical norms have a relation not only in oneself but also with the family and his fellow human. In this chapter, the author has also drawn attention to intervention with others in Khasi Society which brings changes today. Important agents of transformation, impact of British colonialism, the collision with Christianity, globalisation is also given. Each section has a vivid description of the Khasi society where the author has taken the excerpts to understand Khasi matrilineal society with the support statements that he has made that some changes have taken place due to a number of factors. His findings show that many moral, ethical values and norms are eroding; and in a day to day transaction, the power of patriarchy operating in the system which ultimate leads to serious problems and one of those problems is domestic violence. The Second chapter deals with the conceptualizing and contextualizing Domestic violence. The author divides this chapter also into different sections; he starts the chapter with an introduction followed by defining and understanding Domestic Violence in general and mentions the types/forms of domestic violence. The chapter also gives the factors accelerating domestic violence. The author gives the real situation of domestic violence in India and the implementation of the law and the IPC sections to punish the perpetrators and also introduced Domestic violence Act, 2005 for protection from domestic violence. The author in his findings shows that Domestic violence is a global issue; he argues that the notion of patriarcy and its related ideologies help perpetrating violence against women. The author has seen that crime against women is on the rise and is of the view that there is an urgent need to take responsible and constructive action to challenge the rise of Domestic violence. The Third chapter deals with analysing domestic violence in Khasi matrilineal society. The author has again divided this chapter into different sections; beginning with his view that domestic violence is a global issue and as it happens in the patriarchal society it can also happen in the matrilineal socity as well as it is not a phenomenon of the patriarchal society alone. The author tries to analyse this issue pertaining to Khasi matrilineal society. As I have mentioned in the beginning, on the perception that women in the Khasi matrilineal society is enjoying their rights and do not face discrimination which in fact is just a make believed theory but in reality, they too face domestic violence and other crimes against them. Based on the samples collected from different localities of Shillong, Sohra, Mawsynram the author has supported his claim that there is domestic violence in the Khasi society in women as the victims and in rare cases it happens to men also. The author in the description of the samples finds out that in the Khasi matrilineal society women are the main targets of Domestic violence; thus, this reverses the common belief that in the matrilineal society, women enjoy a much better status and are more respected than their counterparts in the patriarchal societies. The author is of the opinion that the discussion on domestic violence needs to be addressed deeply in a more beffitting manner. Justice, equality and liberation through right relationship in the society and family is the dictum where the author feels is the focal point if we are to talk of an inclusive society free of discrimination and violence against fellow human. The Fourth chapter is on the analysis of the basic tenet of the Khasis, *Kamai ïa ka Hok* (Earn righteousness): Towards an indigenous ethical response to domestic violence. The author has defined and conceptualized the term *Kamai ïa ka Hok* and also has given the Khasi understanding of *Ka Hok* and the notion of *Ka Hok* is understood from the creation myth *U Sohpetbneng* literally means the navel of heaven. In giving a clear understanding of *Kamai ïa ka Hok*, the author corelates it with the other two ethical norms *Ka Tipbriew Tipblei* (Know human know God) and *Ka Tipkur Tipkha* (Know one's maternal and paternal relations) by taking excerpts from the writings of renowned Khasi indigenous writers. What makes this chapter more significant is the explanation about *Kamai ïa ka Hok* vis-avis Domestic violence where *Kamai ïa ka Hok* has shaped the social, ethical and theological thinking of the Khasis. The author says it incorporates in its corpus the notion of justice, right relationship and liberation. These therefore act as a response to any unjust and oppressive structure in the society or family. On the other hand, domestic violence is one of the issues that have stained the present Khasi society in any way. The author is of the opinion that violent is an outcome of unjust, bias and oppressive form of relationship. The author, at the end of the chapter has given the suggestions by attempting to give a viable theological-ethical response to the problems of domestic violence to the Khasi matrilineal society. He says *Kamai ïa ka Hok* can act as an interlocutor through which the Khasi culture and Christianity can come together and responding to issues like domestic violence, the church is therefore called to recapture and reinterpret those concepts, which are otherwise also being neglected by the present Khasi generation. Other suggestions are also given in this chapter which I leave to the readers to find it themselves what the author has meaningfully suggested to maintain the right relationship in the family and the society specifically to what the basic tenet *Kamai ïa ka Hok* envisages. The Concluding chapter is the summarisation of the previous chapter along with the findings found by the author on the existence of domestic violence in the Khasi matrilineal society. The author proposes for an indigenous theological-ethical response on how the concept *Kamai ïa ka Hok* is employed as a theological-ethical frame to evolve criteria in order to create a feasible reaponse and counteract domestic violence in the Khasi matrilineal society.

After reading the manuscript, I would definitely comment that this is a very significant work as the author had done an indepth study in analysing how domestic violence exists in Khasi Matrilineal society. With his emperical research established through samples he had chosen, the writer could give a description for finding the accurate results. Since the study focusses on Domestic violence and matrilineal society, the research shows that Khasi women too face different types of domestic violence because of many factors. The existence of patriarchy in the matrilineal society cannot be denied. As I am searching for the right words to include in this foreword, I find myself that I am reviewing the whole manuscript and examining it as an indepth critical research which I did not intend to do so. All I have to say is the work is a meaningful one so I congratulate Rev. Malwin Stone Passah and give the glory to God for giving us the farsighted scholar who speaks for the Khasi society and addresses the concern on the rise of domestic violence in the Khasi society.

I therefore, am really thankful to Rev. Malwin Stone Passah for taking this challenging task to bring out this kind of research that the Khasi society in particular and other readers, researchers, teachers and students in general who want to know the reality of Khasi Matrilineal system will find with perplexity of the existence of domestic violence and the erosion of ethical values in the Khasi society. The book will no doubt benefit readers and looking forward to launching of this new book soon.

Last but not the least, I wish the author the best of luck as he is serving human, he is glorifying God with the blessings that the Almighty has given him. May his talent and hardwork show his caliber to publish more such works in the years to come.

God bless you,

Streamlet Dkhar

That the book in its original form is the thesis submitted to the Senate of Serampore College (University), towards the M.Th. degree and is published with written permission. The researcher is responsible for the title, contents and opinions expressed in it.

ABSTRACT

Domestic violence is a global issue today crossing across barriers of caste, class, status, religion and culture. The Indian society is facing the worst affect of domestic violence. It is understood that the victims are mostly women owing to the patriarchal nature of the society. Nevertheless, this is not just the phenomenon of patriarchal society alone, women in matrilineal society like that of the Khasi in Meghalaya face this malady too. The problem that the researcher observes is that, the common supposition rules out domestic violence in Khasi matrilineal society as it assumed that women enjoy better status and opportunities than their counterparts in patriarchal societies. However, when it comes to day to day transactions it posits numerous problems such as gender differences, interplay of class, status, patriarchy and power, of which domestic violence against women is one of the effects. Therefore, though Khasi society is matrilineal in nature it mirrors a patriarchal society in many ways and domestic violence is a dilemma that the Khasi society is facing today.

In order to interrogate this problem, the researcher collected the data through questionnaires and conducted interviews for a comprehensive view on the subject. The data are analyzed and interpreted following a quantitative method of research. The research reveals that women are the main victims of domestic violence in the Khasi matrilineal society. Nonetheless, men also in subtle ways are victimized. But, the intensity and forms of violence suffer by women are much more in comparison to men. The main types of domestic violence faced by women are physical, verbal, emotional and sexual.

The study also exposes that the important factors causing domestic violence are alcoholism, poverty/unemployment, extra-marital affairs, shift from joint to nuclear family system and patriarchy. The researcher argues that, patriarchy and power in terms of domination are the key ideological and psychological factors which cause domestic violence against women in the Khasi matrilineal society. This has a repercussion on children who are being victimized in the process. Apart from this, the research also discloses that the government, various NGO's and even the church have not played a significant role to counter this problem. Therefore, an immediate concrete and viable response is deemed necessary.

The researcher proposes an indigenous ethical response in which the Khasi concept *Kamai ia ka Hok* (earn righteousness) is employed for evolving certain criteria in order to respond to the above problem. *Kamai ia ka Hok is* a religious-ethical teaching on which the Khasi society is premised upon. It advocates justice, equality and stresses on maintenance of right relationship between human-human and God-human dimensions. It sprang out of the idea that right relationship with fellow human beings is right relationship with God. Therefore, the Khasis emphasize on earning or striving for righteousness through good deeds in terms of justice and equality, which ushers into liberation of human from all clutches of injustices and oppressions. The researcher focuses on the aspects of justice, equality and right relationship between man and woman as criteria to counteract domestic violence in the Khasi matrilineal society. These are the standards which envisage a liberated community of men and women created in the image of God. *Kamai ia ka Hok* also challenges patriarchy and androcentric power which justifies domination, oppression and violence against women. Therefore, it offers a new interpretation of power as relational or shared power which gives direction toward a society or family of equal and liberated partners.

The researcher anticipates that this study will persuade the Khasi society in general and church in particular to counteract domestic violence in a more tangible manner. At the same time, it also operates as a way to conscientize the church to re-capture and re-interpret the meaning and implications of the Khasi indigenous concepts which are slowly diminishing from the present Khasi society.

LIST OF ABBREVIATIONS

AIWC : All India Women's Conference
BD : Bachelor of Divinity
CLS : Christian Literature Society
CSWO : Civil Society Women Organization
DSWO : District Social Welfare Officer
e.g. : example
EKHD : East Khasi Hills District
et al. : and others
etc. : and others
IAW : International Alliance of Women
ICRW : International Center for Research on Women
i.e.: that is to say
IPC : Indian Penal Code
ISPCK : Indian Society for Promoting Christian Knowledge
MSWC : Meghalaya State Women Commission
MTh : Masters of Theology
NCRB : National Crimes Record Bureau
NE : North East
NEN : North East Network
NFHS : National Family Health Survey
NGO's : Non Governmental Organizations
no., nos : number, numbers

n.p.	:	no place of publication given
PCN	:	Peitngor Cable News
PWDVA	:	Protection of Women from Domestic Violence Act
UN	:	United Nations
VAW	:	Violence Against Women
WCC	:	World Council of Churches

LIST OF TABLES

22. Local Durbar (Council) and Domestic Violence.
23. Reasons why local durbar (council) do not take active part in cases of Domestic Violence.
24. Law and Domestic Violence.
25. Men as Victims of Domestic Violence.
26. Role of the Media in Countering Domestic Violence.
27. Role of the Government in Combating Domestic Violence.
28. Role of the Non Governmental Organizations in Fighting Against Domestic Violence.
29. Role of the Church in responding to Domestic Violence.
30. Reasons why the Church do not play a role in opposing Domestic Violence.

INTRODUCTION

1. Statement of the Problem

The Khasi society practices the matrilineal system, in which descent and lineage is traced from the mother's side. The matrilineal system seems to guarantee the rights to women and accord them a higher status. But, when it comes to day to day transactions, it posits enormous problems such as gender difference; inter play of power, patriarchy and status, thus, leading to diverse forms of domestic violence. Therefore, domestic violence is one of the key issues that the Khasi matrilineal society is facing today. Despite Khasi society being matrilineal in nature it reflects the characteristics of a patriarchal society such as domestic violence against women, which is an important dimension of the research. The other dimension is that in the above system, men have also become victims of the same. Violence, whether domestic, or in any other form, is not merely a criminal act of physical force perpetrated against the other person. It covers the whole gamut of exploitation, discrimination, maintaining unequal structures and creation of an atmosphere of terror and threat, all of which are supported by the context of power relations.[1] An attempt therefore, will be made to interrogate the causes and consequences of the above issue pertaining to the Khasi matrilineal society.

---

[1] U. Vindhya, "Battered Conjugality: The Psychology of Domestic Violence", in Kalpana Kannabiran ed., *The Violence of Normal Times* (New Delhi: Women Unlimited Publication, 2005), 197.

Further, taking the social setting of the Khasi society into consideration, the researcher intends to investigate, analyze and interpret the aforementioned problem. Effort will also be made to respond from an indigenous theological-ethical perspective. In the process the research would pursue in motivating the church and society to take up the issue constructively and meaningfully

2. Previous Research

There has been no in-depth research conducted on domestic violence in the Khasi matrilineal society. However, while making a survey of the previous researches, the researcher came across the work of Bornwell Wankhar, *Patriarchy in the Matrilineal of the Khasi: A Christian Response with Special Reference to the Interest of* ***Women's*** *Liberation* (Unpublished M.Th Thesis, Senate of Serampore, 2005). In this work the author emphasizes on the existence and dimensions of Patriarchy within the Khasi matrilineal society. The attempt of the researcher is to prove that patriarchy as an androcentric ideology operates strongly in the matrilineal system against women. This nullifies the common belief that women enjoy a better status in the matrilineal system. On the other hand, the present research emphasizes on proving the fact that domestic violence especially against women is not a phenomenon of patriarchal society alone but the malady of the Khasi matrilineal society. It may also be inferred that, in the same system in subtle ways men are also victimized. Nevertheless, the intensity of violence differs and women are the majority and the main targets of domestic violence. Hence, it attempts to investigate the extent and intensity of domestic violence pertaining to the Khasi matrilineal society. The interplay of power and patriarchy may be looked upon as the key factors that contribute to the rise of domestic violence in the Khasi society.

3. Scope and Limitation

This research is entirely concentrated on the Violence between the spouses or marital partners. It may be argued that in most cases women are the main targets of violence, considering the fact that patriarchy acts as a tool of domination and subjugation of women at the societal and familial levels. Therefore, domestic violence would many a time be referred as the violence against women in their homes. But, in some forms domestic violence against men may not be ruled out completely. However, the amount of domestic violence against women is more rampant in the Khasi society. Therefore, the research will focus primarily on domestic violence against women. It will not deal on the violence on children, old aged and maid/ male servants. The work is confined to the Khasi matrilineal society, within the district of East Khasi Hills, Meghalaya.

4. Method of Research

The research will incorporate library sources and empirical study. The researcher will make use of the available books in various libraries which relate to the subject of Khasi matrilineal society and domestic violence. The empirical nature of the research will follow a quantitative method which is based on the measurement of amount applicable to phenomena that can be expressed in terms of quantity. Interviews and questionnaires will be used to accumulate information. The research was conducted by distributing 75 questionnaires to people who hail from different categories and classes in Shillong city and two villages of Sohra and Mawsynram. The data are analyzed, interpreted and evaluated on the basis of the information collected. In addition interviews were conducted with the heads of local durbars, prominent persons who have vast knowledge on the field concerned and persons related to various NGO's working on the issue of domestic violence.

Having analyzed the data, the researcher will use the Khasi concept *Kamai ia ka Hok* (earn righteousness) as an overarching theological-ethical frame by evolving a set of criteria to evaluate and response to domestic violence from a theological-ethical perspective.

5. Definition of Key Term

The researcher uses the term 'indigenous' instead of 'tribal'. The opinion is that the term 'tribal' implies a derogative meaning. It is most of the time interpreted to mean 'ignorant', 'naked', 'forest dwellers', 'barbaric' etc. Furthermore, the researcher poses some pertinent questions, who is a tribal? and what is tribalism? There are no sufficient answers to these questions. On the other hand, the term 'indigenous' is more inclusive and acceptable in nature. According to the New Shorter Oxford English Dictionary the term 'indigenous' means born in a particular land or region, pertaining to, or concerned with the native inhabitants of a specific place.[2] Therefore, it signifies a particular people who are the inhabitants of a particular geographical area. The researcher uses the word `indigenous' to refer to the Khasis. A Khasi indigenous thinking would mean the worldview of the Khasi as an indigenous people of Meghalaya, India. Thus, the term Khasi indigenous is preferable to Khasi tribal.

6. Structure of the Research

The first chapter presents an overview of the Khasi Matrilineal society. It is an attempt to examine the social, political, cultural, economic and religious dimensions in which the Khasi society is premised upon. The focus is on the socio-cultural aspect particularly focusing on family on which the research revolves upon. The second chapter deals with the conceptualizing and contextualizing domestic violence in India. The intention is to define and conceptualize domestic violence. This is done firstly, by studying the various forms/types of domestic violence and the factors which perpetrate violence in the family; secondly, effort is made to study its intensity in India and a note on law and domestic violence is also included to give a clearer picture on the subject matter. The third chapter focuses on analyzing domestic violence pertaining to the Khasi matrilineal society. It gives a vivid depiction of how domestic violence has affected the Khasi society. This is done by analyzing and interpreting the data collected through questionnaires and interviews. The fourth chapter is an attempt of the researcher to develop certain theological-ethical criteria to response to the above problem. It is being done by using the Khasi concept *Kamai ia ka Hok* (earn righteousness) as a key source to evolve theological-ethical values to counteract domestic violence in the Khasi matrilineal society. The opinion of the researcher is to challenge the Khasi society and church to resurrect this concept which is slowly diminishing from the Khasi worldview, and to give a new impetus for its implications to the society as a whole.

[2] Lesley Brown, ed., *The New Shorter Oxford English Dictionary,* vol 1 (Oxford: Clarendon Press, 1993), 1350.

Chapter 1

KHASI SOCIETY: AN OVERVIEW

Introduction

The Khasi society is accepted globally to be one of the few matrilineal societies in the world. It has its own uniqueness on the basis of the existing system. Like many societies it is premised on certain principles, norms and traditions which shaped its socio-political, economic, cultural and religious dimensions. This chapter attempts to give an overview of the Khasi society in its original form and some of the changes that have taken place over the years. Furthermore, *effort* will be made to focus more on the socio-cultural dimension on which the present research revolves on. Nevertheless, other aspects will also be considered in order to offer a comprehensible view on the Khasi society.

1.1. Defining the Term "Khasi"

The term "Khasi" is a very unique term. It has a particular significance. There has been no general consensus among scholars with regard to the coinage of the term. Khogphai defines "Khasi" as person born of a Khasi mother.[1] This is not so satisfactory as every person is born of a mother. Still further, Bareh opines that *Kha* means born of and

[1] Cf. A. Khongphai, *Principle of Khasi Law* (Shillong: n.p., 1974), 1.

Si which refers to an ancestress.[2] This may sound interesting as the Khasi traced their lineage from the side of the mother. Nevertheless, it falls within the same understanding as the former one. Again Bareh in another version identified the Khasi with indigenous people of Laos and Vietnam.[3] Rodborne is of the view that the term "Khasi" is derived and developed from the Khasi word *sla tyrpad* and *lasi,* bay leaf of which the Greek called it *Kasi* while the English called the same "cassis" that led the Greek historian Ptolemy in 150 AD to mention that the best "Kasi" in the world is produced in South East Asia, North East India.[4] This may be another evidence of the origin of the term "Khasi", but, it has not been able to give a concrete answer to the question who is a Khasi? This may be the reason why the term "Khasi" is unique in itself.

1.2. The Khasi

The Khasi people are a hill tribe inhabiting the Khasi and Jaintia Hills of Meghalaya. They prefer to call themselves as *Ki Hynniew Trep,* which means "the seven huts" or the seven families.[5] The *Hynniew Trep*

---

[2] H. Bareh, *History and Culture of Khasi People* (Guwahati: Spectrum Publication, 1997), 10.

[3] H. Bareh, *A Short History of Khasi Literature* (Shillong: Ri Khasi Press, 1970), 2.

[4] Cf., T. Rodborne, *U Khasi* (Shillong: Ri Khasi Press, 1979), 7-8.

[5] This is derived from a Khasi myth. According to this myth, it is believed that God at first created sixteen families and made them stay with him/her in heaven. They have the freedom to go between heaven and earth by means of a golden ladder, called *Ka Jingkieng Ksiar,* which touched the top of the peak named *Sohpetbneng,* meaning "the navel of heaven". A time came when the seven families expressed the desire to remain on earth. God granted their wishes, but, had to remove the ladder, since then the seven families known as *Ki Hynniew Trep* remained on earth. The other nine families remained in heaven. Thus, there were no longer any movements between heaven and earth since then. The stretch of land that is now called Khasi and Jaintia Hills is usually called the land of seven huts, deriving its name from the people who dwell in it who are known as *Ki khun u hynniewtrep* (children of the seven huts). Originally from the days of old, only one type of people settled in this area. They are called the 'Khasis'. The Jaintias or Pnars as we call them today are only a name invented by the British in pursuit of their policy of `divide and rule'. By differentiating the Khasi from the Pnars they have created a dangerous gap that would harm the solidarity of the people. Thus, the khasi and Jaintias are only one

consist of seven groups, ethnically is of the same people. These are the *Khynriam,* inhabiting the middle uplands, the *Pnar* who live in Jaintia Hills, the *War* who inhabit the deep valleys and hillsides in the south, the *Bhoi* who live on the lowland of the north, the *Maram,* who are on the plateau on the west, the *Lyngngam and the Dyko* inhabit the border of Garo Hills.[6] All these groups of people are known by the name Khasi, which is more or less an umbrella term. They have a specific socio-cultural life and follow the matrilineal system of society.

1.3. The Socio-Cultural Dimension

The Khasi society in the past emphasized on certain norms based on its traditional religion and culture.[7] Culture is the design for living held by members of a particular society. Since humans have no instincts to direct actions, behavior must be based upon guidelines that are learnt from the past.[8] In the same way, we can argue, that,

---

race of people. *Hynniewtrep is* a name applicable to both the groups. Refer, Barnes L. Mawrie, *Introduction to Khasi Ethics* (Shillong: DBCIC Publications, 2005), 12-13.

[6] Cf., Bareh, *The History and Culture of Khasi People...*, 10-11.

[7] For instance, the Khasi traditional religion emphasizes on the three teachings also known as the tenets of Khasi religion, which are thought to govern the life of the people in the society. These teachings are, *Kamai ia ka hok* (earn righteousness), *Tip briew tip blei* (know fellow human know God) and *Tip kur tip kha* (knowing one's maternal and paternal relations). These principles or teachings are like the yardsticks of the society in many aspects whether in the family or outside it. Apart from these, there are other traditional teachings and concepts, which govern the familial and societal life in many ways. Some of these are still adhered and many have also disappeared or are on the verge of disappearing with the changes that have taken place over the years. A detailed discussion on these teachings or norms will be made in the next section.

[8] Michael Haralambos and Robin Heald, *Sociological Themes and Perspective* (Delhi: Oxford University Press, 1980), 3. Edward B. Taylor views culture as that complex whole which includes knowledge, belief, morals, laws, customs and other capabilities and habits acquired by human as members of the society. Yogendra Singh, further opines, that, culture as a unique human reality. It emanates from the unity of human kind in nature, but it situates itself as Meta natural reality. It is manifested in the technological, mental, moral, social, aesthetic and spiritual achievements of human kind. Culture gives meaning to our relationship with others, as it also forms our subjective identity. Therefore, according to him, culture also plays a role in

the Khasi society also has operated through the cultural teachings or principles of the past that are being transferred and followed from one generation to the other. This chapter is an attempt to look at some of the socio-cultural aspects, on which the Khasi matrilineal society is premised.

1.3.1. Matrilineal System

In order to understand the matrilineal system it is better that we see the differences and commonness with the patrilineal system. Many scholars are of the view that if the descent is reckoned from the fathers to the son's sons, the system is patrilineal but if the descent is reckoned from the mother to the daughter to daughter's daughters, the system is matrilineal. However, according to Schneider both Patriliny and Matriliny have three things in common. They are (i) in both, unilineal descent groups are exogamous, (ii) women, have the primary responsibility for the care children and (iii) men have authority over women and children.[9]

The Khasi society is accepted to be a matrilineal society, but there has been confusion as to whether it is matrilineal or matriarchal. The confusion arises because of scholars' opinion. Gurdon states, "The most important and probably the most important characteristics of the Khasi is the observance of matriarchate."[10] Commenting on this confusion, Chowdhury says, "The unfortunate use of the term `matriarchy' originally by Gurdon created a lingering confusion which often stands in the way of a proper appreciation of the ubiquitous and unwavering matrilineal principal underlying the Khasi society."[11]

---

giving identity to the individuals as members of a particular community. Also see, Yogendra Singh, *Culture Change in India: Identity and Globalization* (New Delhi: Rawat Publications, 2000), 25.

[9] Cf. David M. Schneider and Kathleen Gough, eds., *Matrilineal Kinship* (California: University of California Press, 1961), 5.

[10] P.R.T. Gurdon, "Khasis," *Encyclopedia of Religion and Ethics,* edited by James Hastings, vol. 7 (New York: Charles Scribner's Sons Publication, 1955), 690-692.

[11] J.N. Chowdhury, "Kin (clan) in relation to Khasi Matriliny, Land Ownership and village organization," in *Tribal Institution of Meghalaya,* edited by

Bareh says:

> In its original form, Khasi society is a matrilineal not matriarchal since the woman had no right to participate in the acts of legislation, administration and judiciary though a woman was legitimate custodian of family rites and the keeper of the house in normal cases but even she acted under safeguards.[12]

According to Pakyntein:

> The Khasi society is one of the few matrilineal society groups of the world whose social structure is more or less intact. A distinctive feature of Khasi society is the matrilineal principle of descent, succession and inheritance. In descent and inheritance the line passes from mother to daughter, but succession to political offices is from maternal uncle to sister's son.[13]

Further, though the descent is traced through the female, the married woman is subordinate to her husband. In matters of government, it was entirely for the men folk who govern, and the *durbars* were attended mainly by men. In religious ceremonies men played the major role, and the priests *(Lyngdoh)* were generally male.[14] The management of the house and inheritance is purely matrilineal in form. In the opinion of Bareh, the matrilineal system of today should be connected with the long period of migration and the first stage of settlement of the first Khasi in the land. There is evidence from the fact that many mothers in ancient nomadic life

---

S.K. Chattopadhyay (Guwahati: Spectrum Publication, 1985), 140.

[12] Hamlet Bareh, *The History and Culture of Khasi People...*, 337-338.

[13] Valentina Pakyntein, "The Khasi clan: Changing Religion and its Effect," in *Kinship and Family in the North East,* edited by J.S. Bhandari (Delhi: Cosmo Publication, 1996), 349.

[14] The repercussion of this is seen in the Khasi Church. Even after the advance of Christianity, we see the Church still practicing the same principle, where only the males are allowed to conduct religious ceremonies and other important activities. Till today, women were not allowed to enter the altar (in some churches) and they are not ordained into the church ministry.

were considered founders of a number of Khasi clans and folk-kins which have sprung up under their care and guidance while male were their able partners and advisers in the family. He further argues that it is in the Khasi society, we see the most original matrilineal system at work.[15] Still further, Kharlukhi argues that the Khasi society adopted the matrilineal system after they have entered their present homeland. He opines that it has to be adopted so because the land where the khasi entered was covered with thick jungles. People had to clear them and were in constant danger of being attacked by wild animals. It might also be that the men folk were frequently away from home hunting and fighting in wars and likely to be killed. In order to ensure the survival of the community women folk had to stay at home. This, therefore, might have led to the adoption and practice of tracing the line from the mother's side.[16]

1.3.2. Clan System

One of the unique features of the Khasi society is the *Kur* or the clan system that characterizes the structure of the society. It is the first social entity around which other social institutions revolve.[17] These clans are again divided into sub-clans called *Ka Kpoh,* literally meaning `the womb', therefore, having the same ancestral mother. The Khasi are grouped into clans; each clan has its triad, i.e., *Ka Iawbei,* which means the ancestral mother, *U Suidnia,* which means the ancestral maternal uncle of the clan and *U Thawlang,* which means the ancestral father, the progenitor. In each family, a maternal uncle who is considered as the head of the clan occupies a highly respected position; he manages and takes care of all the matters of the family connected with the clan, both material and religious. The father in a Khasi family has no right to meddle with the religious and material affairs of his wife's clan, however, when it comes to his

---

[15] Bareh, *The History and Culture of the Khasi People...,* 33.

[16] B.R. Kharlukhi, "Syiemship in the Khasi Hills Up to 1858 A D" (Unpublished Ph. D Thesis, Gauhati University, 1980), 6.

[17] Helen Giri, "Social Institutions among the Khasi with special reference to the Kinship, Marriage, Family life and Divorce," in *Tribal Institutions of Meghalaya,* edited by S.K. Chattopadhyay (Guwahati: Spectrum Publications 1985), 159-172, here 159.

own clan, he enjoys the privilege as a maternal uncle. This structure of clan system still exists in the present Khasi society and the whole set of relationships revolves around it. Even after the coming of Christianity, the *Kur* or the clan system continues to prevail very strongly.

1.3.3. The Family

The family constitutes the basic social unit of the Khasi society. The family is the foundation of the clan or *Kur* and the whole society. The word family or *Ïng* has two connotations in this context. Firstly, it may refer to a nuclear unit of a father, mother and children as more commonly understood today. Secondly, it may also mean a kinship group comprising of two, three or more *Ïng* (families) who are actually descendants from the womb or *Kpoh* of one mother, grandmother or an ancestress.

In the past when the Khasi families followed the joint family system, the family members would meet around the hearth. It is used often by the elders as a place to educate the young members about specific ways of life and about the etiquettes that should be maintained for a healthy relationship with people and with God.[18] However, this trend seems to have disappeared today with the inclination of the Khasi towards modern lifestyle. Thus, nuclear families are on the rise and the family members do not pay much attention to the customs and practices of the past.

1.3.3.1. Family Organization

Functionally *Ka Ïng* or family comprises of the mother, the brother or maternal uncle and the father and the children. Sometimes it may also include widowed and divorced members.[19] As noted earlier, the families originating from the same mother or ancestress is called *Ka Kpoh* (womb). The *Kpoh* within a certain degree of relationship form *Ka Kur* (clan). The families having a direct lineage on the mother's line are called *Ka Kur Ka Jait*, and those on the father's side are

---

[18] *Ibid.*, 169.

[19] Soumen Sen, *Social and State Formation in Khasi-Jaintia Hills* (Delhi: B.R. Publishing Corporation, 1985), 81-82.

called *Ki Kha Ki Man,* or cousins. *Ka Jait Ka Kynja* stands for all the members of the clan, and the Khasi society is made up of all those clans.[20] The Khasi family is centered on the mother, where her children adopt the mother's clan. Bareh says "the family organization centers around the mother in which capacity she acts as a keeper of the hearth and kitchen and of the Khasi home possessing the authority over property."[21]The mother is the bond of unity and on her death; the youngest daughter assumes the role in organizing the house and relations with members of her kith and kin, therefore, she is also referred to as *Ka Nongri Ïng* or the keeper of the house. The residential house of the mother is termed as *Ïng Seng.*[22] Other brothers and sisters are called *Nongmih Ïng* or the outgoing ones after marriage. They leave the house with their partners and set up a separate dwelling for themselves. A part of the property they secured from their mother is merged with their separate earnings termed as *Nongkhynraw* (self acquired property earned by an unmarried person) and this is passed on to their children. This practice is very much followed in the modern Khasi society.

1.3.3.2. Role of Family Members

In the Khasi family both the mother, father and children have their respective roles to play. The specific role that each member takes up is important for maintaining some sort of an order whether in the family or society at large. For all practical purposes, the intention is not to create a division of labor on the basis of hierarchy, but roles are assigned for the smooth functioning of the family life.

---

[20] Bhusan B. Jatanta, "Changing Khasis: A Historical Account," in *The Tribes of North East India,* edited by S. Karotemprel (Shillong: Centre for Indigenous Cultures, 1998), 336.

[21] H. Bareh, *The History and Culture of the Khasi People...,* 321.

[22] Chowdhury calls this as the "centre of family rituals" where the bond of kinship through a female line that stresses on solidarity is reinforced by the religious association of the *Ing*or the natal home of origin. See, J.N. Chowdhury, "Kin (Clan) in relation to Khasi Matriliny...," 140.

1.3.3.2.1. Role of the Mother or Wife

On account of the matrilineal system among the Khasi, the mother is a person entrusted with the important duties of performing family rites and ceremonies and occupies a position of a family priestess. However, her position is not supreme. Bareh comments, "In the Khasi tradition, a woman is *Ka Nongri Ïng*", that is, the keeper of the house (custodian or trustee).[23]

The woman is considered as *Ka Blei Ïng* (goddess of the house) and *Ka Lukhimai* (the guardian spirit of the house).[24] The names suggest not only the moral attributes of virtue, purity and goodness usually ascribed to a woman, but also her role in the maintenance of the continuity and the growth of her family, her sub clan and her own clan. Furthermore, the Khasi stresses the centrality of the woman in the process of reproduction therefore; she is seen as the centre of the family. She is expected to be fully responsible for the nurturance and care of her children. She is also the repository of family honor.[25] The daughters are the custodians of the family honor and continuity of family line depends on them.

1.3.3.2.2. Role of the Father/ Husband/ Maternal Uncle

The role of the father, husband and maternal uncle[26] is actually played by the same person. The father is the father of his children in

[23] James Poonthuruthil, "The Christian Impact on the Khasi Family," in *The Catholic Church in North East India, 1890-1990,* edited by S. Karotemprel (Shillong: Vendrame Institute, 1993), 441.

[24] Cf., Junita War, "Status of Women in Traditional Khasi Culture," in *Women in Meghalaya,* edited by Somen Sen (Delhi: Daya Publishing House, 1997), 13-14.

[25] Cf., Tiplut Nongbri, "Gender and the Khasi Family Structure, some implications of the Meghalaya succession to Self- Acquired Property Act 1984," *The Sociological Bulletin* 37/122 (March-September 1998): 75-82, here 75.

[26] The role of maternal uncle is under scrutiny today. On account of changing family pattern from joint to nuclear, he tends to play an active role in his own home, with his wife and children, and therefore, cannot take the added responsibility of taking care of his sister's home. It may also be said that due to the *Diaspora* of the Khasi clans caused by urbanization, inter-marriages, search for better employment, education and the other better facilities, the role of the *Kñi* is bound to suffer. In the modem context where the clan members are dispersed to every part of Khasi and Jaintia Hills and even outside, it is no longer possible for the *Kñi* to

his wife's house; he is the maternal uncle of his nieces and nephews in his sister's house.

As stated above, a man belongs to two different houses, that is, *U Kñi* or maternal uncle to his mother's kin and *U Kpa* or father in his wife's home.[27] The Khasi saying is *"U Kpa uba lah baiai, u kñi uba tip ha ka iap"* (the father bears the heat and burden of the day, the maternal uncle is present only in matter of life and death). In fact, a man and his wife's brother represent the two aspects of a relationship which binds every man in the Khasi society to his mother's house than to his wife's house. Nataranjan comments:

> The grateful expression of the Khasi child *U Kpa u ba lah baiai ia ka long rynieng* (an able father who gives us life and stature) shows that the khasi male is important in his wife's house as he is the one who takes care for the welfare of his children, which is an ample proof of the `de facto' position of the father in the early Khasi family.[28]

To show that a male member in the Khasi family is not without position and power, Bareh quotes the following from Cantlie "...a man can hold self-acquired property *(Nongkhynraw)* but even in some circumstances ancestral property *(Nongtymmen).* Another reason to say that his role and position is not weak or awkward is because the Khasi wife addresses her husband as *Kynrad* (lord)[29] showing that a Khasi male gets respect from his wife in the family.

1.3.3.2.3. Role of Children

The foundation of the Khasi family is not only the father or the mother but most importantly the children. The parents cannot

---

interact with the number of his clan. This therefore has led to the diminishing role of the *Kñi* in the modem Khasi society. Today, the role of the *Paterfamilias* (*u* Kpa) is gradually emerging to substitute that of the *Kni.* The image of the moral displinarian traditionally seen as the *Kni*is today assumed b~ the father of the family. Refer, Barnes L. Mawrie, *Introduction To Khasi Ethics...,* 86-87.

[27] Poonthuruthil, "The Christian Impact on the Khasi Family...," 441.

[28] Nalini Nataranjan, *The Missionary among the Khasi* (New Delhi: Sterling Publishing Ltd., 1997), 19.

[29] Cf., H. Bareh, *The History and Culture of the Khasi People...,* 335.

build their family without possessing children.[30] Children are the assets of the family. Children enjoy a special position in the Khasi family. They are looked upon with love and respect, and there are no illegitimate children in the traditional society. However, the situation has changed tremendously today, where we can see the number of illegitimate children and cases of single parenting are on the rise. The reason for this is because of the loosening bond of marriage, in which men are not bound to certain law or legal mechanism. Most marriages are not recognized by the law. Therefore, this give freedom for the men to leave a woman any time they want to do so, which leads to abandoning of a relationship, leading to severe consequences on the woman herself and the whole family.

The *Khatduh* or the youngest daughter enjoys a privileged position in the Khasi family, where she inherits all the property, including the ancestral property. Nevertheless, she can be only the custodian. In other sense, she is only the caretaker and not the possessor of the family property. She cannot go against the decision of her maternal uncle or family council under whose advice she carries out her duties. In the traditional Khasi society the *Kñi* or maternal uncle controlled and supervised over the ancestral property. But today due to the gradual disappearance of the authority of the *Kñi* the traditional control over the ancestral property is never felt. In fact today, the *Khatduh* or the youngest daughter has become the sole owner of the ancestral property. There is a common practice to dispense of this property as she likes and also to claim ownership over the whole ancestral property.[31] The other brothers and sisters are called *Nongmih Ïng* or outgoing members because they will get married and set up a separate dwelling.[32]

1.3.3.4. Marriage

Marriage for the Khasi is not simply a civil affair but has a religious sanction. They are strictly exogamous. For the Khasi, marriage within

---

30 H. Onderson Mawrie, *Ka Pyrkhat U Khasi* (Shillong: Lyngwiar Press, 1994), 33.

31 Cf., Barnes L. Mawrie, *Introduction to Khasi Ethics...,* 87.

32 Cf., H. Bareh, *The History and Culture of the Khasi People...,* 298.

the clan is a taboo, which cannot be forgiven. Transgressors will be excommunicated from the clan, deprived of the inheritance.[33] Before any marriage both the families make a deep inquiry into the family matters. They strive to uncover all inauspicious circumstances which might bring about desirable consequences or which bring about unpleasant eventualities on *Ka daw ïng.* For an honorable marriage, the boys' side will propose and the girls' family before accepting will consult the omen to ensure there is no *Shongsang* (marriage within the clan). Before the marriage, the boy with his uncles and male relatives will go to the girl's family, which is known as *Pynhiar synjat* or an engagement. But the couples will not be husband and wife till the formal marriage is fixed.[34] Therefore, the Khasi have a custom of prearranged marriage.[35]

Thus, it can be said that, the Khasi believed that the morality of the society depends upon the families. As said earlier the Khasi marriage is a serious matter, therefore, the elders of the family take up the task of organizing marriage. In its original form, the Khasi marriage is arranged by the parents along with the maternal and paternal uncles.[36] But this trend of marriage has changed dramatically in the present days. A public living together of a man and a woman without any ceremony constitutes a valid marriage.[37]

---

[33] *lbid.,* 291.

[34] Cf., G. Costa, *Ka Riti Jong Ka Ri Laiphew Syiem* (Shillong: Don Bosco Publication, 1994), 20. After the marriage, the husband will go to the wife's place. Halfway the bride's uncles and male relatives will welcome the husband and his relatives with the exchange of *Kwai*or betel nuts. A religious ceremony is performed, invoking the blessings of the ancestors and God. The groom will have to stay for three days consecutively in the bride's residence, before taking his wife to his parents.

[35] Barnes L. Mawrie, *Introduction to Khasi Ethics...,* 34.

[36] *1bid.,* 34.

[37] This type of settlement is considered as the most negative influence of westernization on the Khasi society as a whole and particularly to the system of marriage. It has led not only to the degeneration of Khasi marriage but also affects the family life and the society as a whole. The Khasi cultural ethos is put in danger, and the traditions and customs of the past seems to be fast disappearing. Recently, the Khasi Hills Autonomous District Council (KHADC) has passed some legal resolutions with regard to marriage. According to this, the couple who wish to stay together without actually marrying in their religious traditions or even court

1.3.3.5. Divorce

Among the Khasi, divorce is very common because if the man and a woman cannot live happily, they agree to divorce. The common causes of divorce are barrenness, adultery, ill treatment, non-maintenance.[38] If the marriage had been conducted with the knowledge of the clan members, they should also witness the divorce.[39] It is only after that the divorce of any couples becomes valid. When divorce takes place, a ceremony known as *Ka pyllait san shyieng*[40] is performed by both husband and wife in front of the witnesses. Divorce is prohibited among the Khasi during pregnancy for the sole reason that the child to be born would not be *a Khunrei* or an illegitimate child. However, these customs and traditions are gradually disappearing in the present

marriage, would need the consent or the certification of the village headman (sic) who would be the marriage official.

[38] This fact however, should not lead us to think that marriage is a trivial matter among the Khasi. They hold marriage to be very sacred. There are numerous reasons why divorce is practiced. The Khasi generally believe that marriage is the scheme of God for human. A man and a woman come together because God has designed it to be so. Thus a Khasi would undoubtedly expect every couple to live in peace and harmony. If God has willed it, he will fructify this sacred union. Therefore, a marriage that does not bring happy consequences is looked as unfavorable to God. See, Barnes L. Marwie, *Introduction to Khasi Ethics…*, 36.

[39] Giri, "Social Institution...," 170.

[40] Before this event is conducted, a public announcement regarding the divorce and ceremony was done in the whole village. The wife gives five cowries to her husband and he returns to her ten cowries. She then returns them to him which he takes and throws to the ground. Sometimes one party will be unwilling to divorce. In such cases the party desiring the divorce must pay something to the other. When this is done, each party takes its own property and divides the jointly acquired property. Cf. K. Cantlie, *Notes on Khasi Laws* (Shillong: Ri Khasi Press, 1971), 77. In the olden days love marriage were never favored. Marriages were pre-arranged by the parents. Today, pre-arranged marriage has become outdated. According to the old Khasi custom a Khasi male can have two wives, one real wife and the other, a stolen wife *(tngatuh)*. Today, due to the influence of Christian Ethics such a practice is considered improper and sinful. A person can have only one wife. Divorce, though not favored, was never prohibited in the olden days if sufficient reasons were brought forward. But today divorce is not encouraged. Divorce according to the Christian teaching is a great sin. This in turn has tempted many Khasi youth to shun proper marriages for all stipulations involved in them. Cf. Barnes L. Mawrie, *Introduction to Khasi Ethic...*, 88.

Khasi society, whereby, frequent divorce cases take place resulting in many illegitimate children being born into the society. This in return has a tremendous and adverse impact on the families and especially on the social functioning of these children.

1.3.3.6. Inheritance

With regard to the system of inheritance, the guiding principle is to keep the ancestral property in the family entrusting the management and control of it to the brothers of the mother and the custody to the *Khatduh* or the youngest daughter. Inheritance is purely matrilineal in organization. The *Khatduh* or the youngest daughter inherits the property but she is not the sole owner/ possessor of the inherited property.[41] However, she is debarred from such status if she enters into any illegal or unauthorized marriage[42] and this is followed strictly till date. Nevertheless, apart from her, even the other daughters of the family receive their share of inheritance in the form of land, vessels, ornaments, residential houses, tools, implements, etc., but the lion's share is given to the youngest daughter. The main moral consideration regarding the division of property among the Khasi is the concern for the weaker sex. Thus property is usually given to the daughters because they are unable to earn for themselves like the men do.[43] Succession by males takes place when there is no female in the family.[44] In the present society, even sons inherit some of the

---

[41] Cantlie, *Notes on Khasi Laws...*, 77.

[42] Namrita Catherine Shadap, *The Origin and Early History of the Khasi Synteng People* (Calcutta: Firma KLM Private Ltd., 1981), 330.

[43] Th*e Khatduh* or the youngest daughter gets the lion's share not because of partial treatment; rather it is because of a sense of justice pervading the Khasi mind. The *Khatduh* is the guardian of the parents in their old age. She is also the up keeper of family traditions and rites. Her house is frequented by every member of the *Kur* or the clan. All these things imply a lot of expenses on her part. It is precisely because of this fact that the Khasi feel that it is right and just to allot to her a greater portion of the ancestral property. See, Barnes L. Mawrie, *Introduction to Khasi Ethics...*, 34.

[44] There are certain norms regarding this succession. A male successor holds the property only in his life time. His children do not inherit the property, since they belong to the *Kur* or clan of the mother. A male inheritor usually keeps a female from his clan and later on as successor to the property. Successor to the property being a female, he has no right to sell this property even though it may be

property depending on the possessions owned by their family, but this varies from one family to the other.

1.3.3.7. Status of Men and Women

In the traditional Khasi society, men and women have their own status in the family and society at large. Being a matrilineal society where descent is traced from the female side, there seems to be that women enjoy higher status than men. This section will try to unravel this, for further clarity on the subject matter.

1.3.3.7.1. Status of Men

In the Khasi understanding a man is conferred the role of the protector and the provider[45] and this is substantiated by the saying *U Rang khadar buit khadar bor*[46] or a man has twelve strengths and twelve strategies. This statement shows the superiority of man over woman. In the family he has to play a double role, the role of maternal uncle in his sister's house and father to his children. Streamlet Dkhar quoted Gurdon who observe that a Khasi man is the head of the family, the one who supports the family, as said "the one who bears the heat and cold". He further opines that taking mother's clan does not mean the father does not have any part in the affairs of the family.[47] In the religious circle, a Khasi man plays an important role of the one who initiates and conducts the ceremony, and therefore priesthood is most of the time defined as a male vocation. This understanding

---

a moveable property like gold and ornaments. The profits he makes in the landed property can be used by him for the maintenance of his family. Refer, Cantlie, *Notes on Khasi Law...,* 15.

[45] Cf., Bareh, *The History and the Culture of the Khasi People...,* 301.

[46] This statement shows the vivid example of how patriarchy operates in the Khasi society, where men are looked as stronger as and fitter than their women counterpart. Women on the other hand were looked as weaker by a saying *Shibuit shibor,* or a woman has just one strength and one strategy, which shows that women are dependent on men, on account of being weak and vulnerable. This kind of stereotype continues in the present society, where subjugation and discrimination against women is seen in many ways whether in the family or society.

[47] Cf. Streamlet Dkhar, "Ka Kyrdan U Rangbah Khasi," in *Ki Sngi Jong Ngi,* edited by H.W. Sten (Shillong: Don Bosco Press, 1994), 1.

is carried on to the present society, where even after the coming of Christianity, priesthood is looked entirely as the work that only male member can take up.

In the political domain, only male holds public office, in fact politics is a male profession, where men feel that they should be the one to organize and administer public affairs so as to ensure peace and security. Men consider women as weaker sexes who are unable to rule and administer and hence do not allow them to sit in any public council or *durbar.* A woman who dares to voice her opinion in public affairs is regarded as the "hen that crows"- a freak of nature.[48] This stereotypic understanding still continues, where women are still not allowed to attend public meeting or *durbar* even though on the other side women have started to enter into the political realm in the present days.

1.3.3.7.2. Status of Women

In the light of the existing practice of Matriliny among the Khasi, the status of women in the family and social organizations is very important. The woman is considered as *Ka blei Ïng* (goddess of the house) and *Ka Lukhimai* (the guardian spirit of the house). These names suggest not only the moral attributes of virtue, purity and goodness usually ascribed to women, but also their roles in the maintenance of continuity of her family, sub clan and clan.[49] Therefore, she is rightly called *Ka nongbat ka nonglum* (the nurturer and the holder). The Khasi saying *dei jait na ka kynthei* (from the woman sprang the clan) shows that when reckoning descent, count from the mother only, they speak of a family of brothers and sisters who are great grandchildren of one great grandmother, as *shikpoh,*

---

[48] This is a derogative saying against women. Thus, it shows how patriarchy had operated and continues to operate where men are looked as powerful and women as weaker and subordinated. Till the present day in many ways women have no voice in decision making, even though they have become more independent in many ways. The stigmatization and stereotype continue to haunt them in many ways, especially in the very grass root of the society.

[49] Cf., Junita War, "Status of Women in Traditional Khasi Culture," in *Women in Meghalaya,* edited by Somen Sen (Delhi: Daya Publishing House, 1997), 13.

literally translated as one womb.[50] The Khasi mother has special privileges and responsibilities at home. If she is the youngest daughter she is responsible for the ancestral property, which means she is the custodian in the strict sense of the word.

In the political sphere, women consider politics as being men's profession. Therefore, men considered that women should concern with domestic affairs and should not dabble with public affairs.[51] In the traditional Khasi society, it is observed that in view of women' active participation in domestic affairs, they need not occupy state or political offices. Thus, women do not have voting rights in elections to traditional council or offices. Nevertheless, though women have become more independent in the present time, the same stigmatization follows, the fact that very few women are seen in political affairs eventually justify the above understanding.

1.4. Economic Profile

The economy of the Khasi in the past was exclusively based on agricultural products as agriculture was the main occupation. Nevertheless, many changes took place over the years especially with the coming of the Britishers. New ventures in economy were developed through the introduction of cash crop farming, mining and other related industries.

1.4.1. Agriculture

Agriculture was the main occupation of the people and this enhanced the other forms of economic life. In the past, agriculture was entirely concentrated for the reason of subsistence. But the coming of the Britishers brought about the technical know-how, whereby, the Khasi shifted to cash crop farming which has ultimately boosted their economic life. The process of cultivation practiced by the Khasi is both permanent and shifting.[52] The coming of the Britishers in one

---

[50] P.R.T. Gurdon, *The Khasi* (Delhi: Cosmo Publication, 1975), 82.

[51] Cf., M.P. Passah, "Status of Women in Jaintia Society and Culture," in *Women in Meghalaya,* edited by Somen Sen (Delhi: Daya Publishing House, 1997), 52.

[52] Shifting cultivation (Jhumming) was carried on in the past which ultimately leads to deforestation and soil erosion. This process of cultivation is stopped today

way is a blessing, to the whole process of agriculture and enhanced the economic life of the Khasi. New methods of farming were introduced and today, we see cultivation of more cash crops[53] which is aimed for profit making and commercial purposes. Agriculture products are now traded outside the state[54] or even abroad.

1.4.2. System of Land Ownership

The system of land ownership among the Khasi is of two different types: firstly, the private land, known as *Ri Kynti,* and community land, known as *Ri Raid.* Land ownership has its own implications on the society, where in the past everybody in some way or the other has access to the land for survival through cultivation. Today, this is not the case the rich and the powerful only gain access to the land.

1.4.2.1. *Ri Kynti* (Private Land)

Ri Kynti are lands set apart for certain clans upon whom were bestowed the proprietary, heritable and transferable rights over such lands.[55] These lands were sometimes claimed by a particular family or clan by virtue of continued possession and cultivation, which consequently formed their *Ri Kynti.*[56] *Ri Kynti* land is divided into two categories (i) Ancestral and (ii) Self-acquired. The clan has control on the former and the person acquiring has full control over the land in the later. This system of land ownership has led to serious

owing to the ecological problems it caused. This is replaced by a modem cultivation process called terrace cultivation, which helped in preserving the soil.

[53] Main crops cultivated are rice, potato, different kinds of vegetable, rubber, timber, tealeaf, betel nuts, betel leaves. Nowadays, different kinds of flower and fruit are cultivated for commercial purposes. In Ri Bhoi District, sometimes, the same field is cultivated twice in a year, where rice and vegetables like tomato, cauli flower, French beans etc., are cultivated to be sold in the local markets or even exported outside the state also.

[54] P.N. Dutta, *Impacts of the West on Khasi and Jaintias: A Survey of Political and Economic Change* (Delhi: Cosmo Publications, 1982), 160.

[55] W.C. Khongwir, "A Christian Ethical Response to Ecological Problems in the Khasi Hills of Meghalaya" (Unpublished M.Th Thesis, Senate of Serampore College, 1997), 23.

[56] J.N. Chowdhury, *The Khasi Canvas: A Cultural and Political History* (Shillong: Jaya Chowdhury, 1978), 156.

complications today, where it has become the monopoly of the few rich clans, families or persons. So, gaining access to the land is at the hand of the rich and the powerful.[57]

1.4.2.2. *Ri Raid* (Community Land)

Ri Raid is the land belonging to the community as a whole, and a person occupying a Ri Raid has no permanent, heritable or transferable right over it. The management of the land lies within the jurisdiction of the community concerned.[58] However, as time went by, the *Ri Raid* lands were also being transformed into private lands owing to the reason that as long as the people could maintain the land they occupy, it could not be taken away from them.[59] In accordance to this, Chowdhury commented that owing to the ascendancy of private ownership among the Khasis, there exists the capitalist trend to grow rich by augmenting the *Ri Kynti* of a family by purchase of land and by enclosing as much of the *Ri Raid* land as it possibly can.[60] The system of land ownership in the present Khasi society is fast changing. Private ownership of land is encouraged where only

---

[57] This has serious implications on the economic life of poor families or clans. An examination of landownership among traders in Meghalaya shows that only 35 per cent of households own land while the rest (65 per cent) have no land at all. In many households, diminished access to land resulted in a multiplicity of occupations as both men and women turned to various occupations to supplement the decreasing family income. But while there are many low-skilled jobs such as carpentry, masonry, furniture making, motor repairing, and driving available to men, the avenues for women are highly restricted. This means that women either had to reconcile themselves to casual wage labor, which is riddled with uncertainties, or they had to create their own employment opportunities in areas more in tune with their traditional role. Many pavement sellers and small-scale retailers entered the market under these circumstances. See, Tiplut Nongbri, *Gender, Matriliny and Entrepreneurship, the Khasi of North-East India* (New Delhi: Zubaan Publication, 2008), 57.

[58] Chowdhury, *The Khasi Canvas...*, 163.

[59] R.T. Rymbai, "Patterns of Land Holding of the Khasi-Pnars..., 187-194, here 189.

[60] J.N. Chowdhury, "Kur (Clan) in Relation to Khasi Matriliny, Land Ownership and Village Organization," in *Tribal Institutions of Meghalaya,* edited by S.K. Chattopadyay (Gauhati: Spectrum Publications, 1985), 137-159, here 155.

the rich can own land for their vested interests, whereas the poor continue to live without land.

1.4.3. Division of Labour and Wage Policy

In the past, there was no system of land revenue either on the *Ri Kynti* or *Ri Raid* lands according to the customary patterns of land holding system among the Khasi.[61] Thus, division of labour was not an issue in the past, since almost everybody had access to land in order to cultivate. There were gradual changes in this regard, only after the coming of the Britishers, whereby, private ownership of lands was encouraged. The introduction of cash crop farming leads to serious complications, where the rich could own land and cultivate. Therefore, in the present day, we see more of landless workers being as wage labourers with the minimum wage ranging from Rs. 50-70 for women and Rs. 80-100 for men. On the other hand, the recent policy of private entrepreneurship has created some kind of a class orientation in the Khasi society. The whole issue revolves around the question who owns the means of production? If we look critically, it is the elite class represented by certain clans, who have access to the land, controls the economy. Tiplut Nongbri argues that as Khasi society lacked a formal system of stratification, the division between groups was rarely pronounced as it is in other societies. Yet within this broad egalitarian framework, social differentiation is surely and rapidly emerging. Economic inequality and differential access to resources have placed individuals in positions of competition and opposition to each other.[62] The rich family or clan having access to resources automatically occupies the higher position or class and the poor and the landless family or clan becomes the lower or the working class.

1.4.4. Trade Relation

Trade relation or trading is an important aspect in shaping the economic life of the people. The Khasi are good traders. Bareh opines

---

[61] R.T. Rymbai, "Patterns of Land Holding of the Khasi-Pnars...," 190.

[62] Tiplut Nongbri, *Gender, Matriliny and Entrepreneurship, the Khasi of North-East India...*, 68.

that the presence of aged tracts and bridled paths may have afforded the means of communication for promoting and enhancing trade relations. He further says that though the bulk of the populations were agriculturists, there were among them traders, administrators and collectors.[63] The Khasis did not confine to agriculture alone, but in some ways have developed their own idea of trade and commerce to gear up their economic life. Today, with better transport facilities, trading has become very important in terms of enhancing and providing better opportunities for livelihood. Goods like coal, limestone, timber, varieties of fruits and vegetables are exported to different neighboring states and even to Bangladesh.

1.5. Political Structure

In the past, *Syiemship* or kingship and *dolloi ship*or administratorship appears to be the most prevalent system of the Khasi polity. When the administration of *Syiemship* started, many states under the *Syiem* or king as the chief were formed in the Khasi lands. These states constitute what is known as *Raid* (units/ sub units) and villages. O.L. Snaitang identified six elements within the Khasi political system.[64] These are the *Syiem* or chief,[65] *Ki Bakhraw* or the founding clan[66]

---

[63] Bareh, *The History and the Culture of the Khasi People...*, 435.

[64] O.L. Snaitang, *Christianity and Social Change in North- East India* (Shillong: Vendrame Institute, 1999), 14.

[65] The chief is known as *Syiem* or king in the Khasi society. He is the head of the state called *Hima.* The *Syiem is* selected from the ruling clan called *Jait syiem,* which is made of different sub clans and families. The *Syiem is* instrumental in enforcing the decision of the council. He and the cabinet of ministers has to look after the administration which check the proper functioning of market, prisons, extra territorial defense, inter-states affairs and affairs related to people's life and the state. However, although the king holds such powers, the same are constrained. Gurdon writes, "according to customs, he can perform no act of any importance without consulting or obtaining the approval of the assembly/ durbar upon which the ministers sit. Cf., P.R.T. Gurdon, *The Khasis...*, 66.

[66] *Ki Bakhraw* or the founding clans compose of the senior members of the founding clan being the original settlers of the state. Each of these clans select the representative to the state assembly where they serve as political advisers to the king, thereby, occupying a higher status in the society.

Durbar Hima or the state assembly,[67] *Durbar Raid* or the units/ sub units assembly,[68] *Durbar Shnong* or the village assembly[69] and *Durbar Kur* or the clan assembly.[70] These elements make the political and administrational system of the Khasi in the past. However, they began to become less important during the colonial and the post-colonial period. There have been many changes after the Indian

---

[67] The state assembly consists of the *Syiem,* the *Bakhraw* and the representatives of the *Raid* and village councils who come together for the function of the assembly. The ancient Khasi call it *Ka Durbar blei,* which means the divine assembly, believing that God himself (Sic.) is present in the assembly. This is regarded as the supreme authority of the state and is the evidence of the democratic nature of the Khasi polity. The main duty of the assembly is to consolidate the main administration over markets, lands, religious ceremonies, to maintain rights of the people and to strengthen social values. Refer, Snaitang, *Christianity and Social Change...,* 15-16.

[68] The *Raid* are units or sub units of the states. Each *Raid* covers an area of many villages. The head of the *Raid is* the *Rangbah Raid/ Sordar Raid,* who is elected from persons who belong to certain designated clans. The other selected are mostly the village heads except some who act in an advisory capacity. Activities such as settlement of lands for building, cultivation and other works are discussed and resolved in the assembly. The assembly is responsible for distribution of lands to the public for several purposes. Boundary disputes and other public problems are discussed and settled in this assembly. See, Snaitang, *Christianity and Social Change...,* 16.

[69] The village assembly exists in every village and this continued to operate till the present day. Election to the post of *Rangbah Shnong* or the headman of the village may differ from one village to another. It can be hereditary or general. One male member of each family represents the village assembly. The assembly tries in solving cases involving crimes and other related cases. Today, the village assembly is a very important -part of the Khasi society as it has its own rules or laws enacted for the well being of the village or locality.

[70] In the Khasi society, each clan has its own assembly or *Durbar Kur* in which *U Kñi Rangbah* or the eldest maternal uncle acts as the head. The assembly is always held at the original house known as the *Ingseng* which means the house of the ancestral mother of the clan. The assembly has to look after the property of the clan known as *Ri Kur* and to settle any disputes related to the clan. Today, the role of the *Durbar Kur is* not so prominent owing to various reasons. One of the reasons is the constant migration of the clan members to various parts of the state or even outside for the sake of employment opportunities, which therefore make it difficult to meet. Another factor may be the diminishing role of the maternal uncle, which is now replaced by the father of the family. Nevertheless, *Durbar Kur* still exists in some form.

independence; nevertheless, the Khasi traditional polity continues to operate in subtle form till today.

1.6. The Religious Setup

The Khasi religion is also called as *Ka Niam Tip Briew Tip Blei* (a religion that knows God and human beings). The word "religion" in Khasi is represented by the word *Niam.*[71] The Khasi believed that their religion is given by God to human beings for their conduct and has to do much with their daily life. For the Khasis, *Ka Niam* has different implications in their social, political, religious and economical life. In short, religion controls their overall behavior towards God and fellow humans. This principle is premised on certain religious-ethical teachings which serve as the yard stick for their daily living. In other words, these teachings or also called as the tenets of the Khasi religion form the core of the Khasi ethos.

1.6.1. Traditional Religious-Ethical Teachings

The Khasi religion emphasizes on three important aspects which form the core of their social behavior and therefore govern the life of the people in the society. These teachings are, *Kamai ia ka Hok,* literally meaning 'earn righteousness', *Tip Briew tip Blei,* meaning `know human know God' and *Tip Kur tip Kha,* meaning, 'knowing one's maternal and paternal relations. As stated earlier, these teachings have deeper implications on the Khasi milieu and their world view.

1.6.1.1. *Kamai ia ka Hok* (Earn Righteousness)

Kamai means to earn by one's effort and labour; *ia is* a preposition following a transitive verb and governing an object noun; *Ka Hok*

---

[71] The word *Niam* has two fold implications that constitute the primary expression of understanding of religion and human's relationship with God. In the first place, *Niam* comes from two words with different connotations, i.e., *Nia* meaning `reason' and *baim* meaning `living'. Hence, it is *Nia im*or the living reason. Secondly, the term *Niam* implies a larger and deeper connotations meaning *Ka Nia Ka Jutang,* which literally means `the reason the covenant'. Therefore, religion is a covenant, which the Khasi made with God and based on this they also develop their relationship with God and fellow human beings. For detailed discussions refer, Iarington Kharkongor, *Ka Dienshonhi* (Shillong: Self, 1968), 254ff.

means righteousness. So *Kamai ia ka Hok*[72] can be translated literally as earn righteousness.[73]*Ban Kamai ia ka Hok* (to earn righteousness) is a foundation for the life of the Khasis, in order to earn this, he/she has two options, firstly, *Ka jingtip Blei* (to know God), and secondly, *Ka jingtip briew* (to know fellow human). To live a righteous life a person must not only speak the truth and act fairly and justly in all his/her dealings with fellow humans but always strive to be honest in his/her very thoughts and wishes as well. This teaching had shaped the social and ethical principles of the Khasi society in the past; nevertheless, it has slowly deteriorated in the present Khasi society.

1.6.1.2. *Tip* Briew Tip Blei (To Know Human and to Know God)

Tip means 'to know'; *briew* means 'human'; *Blei* means 'God'. So *Tip briew tip Blei* can be literally translated as 'know fellow human know God' or 'human consciousness, God consciousnesses.[74] This teaching stresses that human can only know God when he/she know his/her fellow beings. Knowing his/her fellow beings connote performance of one's duties to them, which is to be good, helpful to one and all: not to cause harm or injury to anyone for one's own profit or pleasure. It is because of this reason the Khasi religion is called *Ka Niam Tip briew tip Blei*[75] (a religion that know or is conscious of human and God). It is believed that a human who does not know or have concern for his/her fellow beings will not reach *Ka Dwar U Blei*[76] (gate of God or heaven). This teaching had served as a yardstick for the social life of the Khasi in the past. Nevertheless, it

---

[72] This concept will be discussed in detail in the later chapter. The attempt of the researcher is to develop and evolve some theological-ethical criteria using the above concept in order to response to domestic violence which is looked as one of the maladies that the present Khasi society is facing today.

[73] Cf., R.T. Rymbai, "Some aspects of the Religion of the Khasi-Pnar," in *Khasi Heritage: A Collection of Essays,* edited by Hipshon Roy (Shillong: Seng Khasi, 1996), 111.

[74] *Ibid.,* 111-112.

[75] Sib Charan Roy, *Ka Niam Tip Briew Tip Blei* (Shillong: Ri Khasi Press, 1919), 12.

[76] Rymbai, "Some aspects of the Religion of the Khasi-Pnar...," 112.

has in some way become less important in the present generation, whereby, it may also disappear soon from the Khasi social, cultural and ethical life. The impact of globalization can be clearly seen in which the traditional values are slowly being eroded and are replaced by a global culture, where changing life styles and values can be explicitly seen.

1.6.1.3. Tip Kur Tip Kha (To know one's Maternal and Paternal Relations)

Kur means maternal relations, *Kha* means paternal relation. So *Tip Kur Tip Kha* means to know one's maternal and paternal relation.[77] The *Tip Kur Tip Kha* is a socio-religious creed on which the sanctity of social relationship is based. It was perceived as the meeting point between the human and the divine. It was a sin to marry within the clan of the mother, and even close relations from the father's side.[78] Those who violate this are looked upon as not as having broken the human rules but the divine command. They are considered as out caste and even their heads shaved in three patches to become fugitive and vagabonds, not daring to show their faces to others.[79] This teaching has shaped the social-ethical values in the past and which continues till the present Khasi society. This in many ways has shaped the understanding of relationship among the Khasi, especially the family ties that prevails in the whole society.

1.7. Khasi Society: Important Agents of Transformation

The Khasi society in many ways has undergone many important changes. These changes have taken place due to some specific events in the history. Notably, the period of British colonialism and the advent of Christianity had made a tremendous impact on the Khasi society.

---

[77] *Ibid.*, 112.

[78] Cf, Snaitang, *Christianity and Social Change in North East India...*, 36.

[79] Rymbai, "Some aspects of the Religion of the Khasi-Pnar...," 112.

1.7.1. Impact of British Colonialism

Hamlet Bareh, an eminent Khasi scholar, opines that, the British colonized the Khasi states in around the year 1824-1826.[80] Prior to the British colonialism, the Khasi were independent people with their own set of culture, belief system and specific sociological outlook. Nevertheless, colonialism has brought about many changes in the social, political, cultural, economical and religious aspects of the Khasi society. Politically, many of the independent states, called *Hima* were either dissolved or assimilated in the British Raj. The traditional Khasi polity gives way to the British idea of governance. Economically, the Khasi society was transformed, as the Britishers introduced the technical know-how in agriculture, where, cash crop farming becomes very prominent. This ushered in the improving economic life of the people. However, the traditional form of farming and land holding system were changed drastically, where, the rich and the powerful then began to gain control and monopoly of land and agriculture. Culturally, the traditional customs, lifestyles, norms and values were undergoing a constant change, impacting the social and cultural fabric of the Khasi society.

1.7.2. Collision with Christianity

R. T. Rymbai asserts that, until the advent of Christianity, the relationship with the British was mostly political and commercial.[81] The coming of the Christian missionaries saw the spread of Christianity and the impact it had on people's life and their world view. There have been many changes that have taken place through varied services, especially education. The advancement in educational opportunities developed a group of people who slowly emerge as a new class represented by the intelligentsia. P.N. Dutta opines that, the intelligentsia formed the most influential group in an age when education was the passport to employment, symbol

---

[80] Bareh, *The History and Culture of Khasi People...*, 11.

[81] R.T. Rymbai, "Evolution of Modem Khasi Society," in *Khasi Heritage*, edited by Hipshon Roy (Shillong: Seng Khasi, 1979), 62.

of status and power, and above all the hallmark of `civilization.[82] Furthermore, Christianity is also criticized for evolving a new culture imitating the lifestyles and culture of the west. Therefore, the advent of Christianity, though has improved the life of the people but at the same time it is also blamed to have eroded the traditional moral and ethical values of the Khasi.

1.7.3. Globalization

Globalization no doubt has impacted the Khasi society in many ways. Barbara Dohling in her thesis, "Interrogating the Importance and Significance of *Tip Briew Tip Blei* (to know People is to know God) for Developing an Ethical Critique of the Contemporary Khasi Society" opines Globalization has brought both positive and negative impact on the Khasi society. On the one hand, it has brought in new technologies like televisions, computers and internet facilities at the doorsteps of the people, thus bringing closeness to the people in other parts of the globe. On the other hand, it also benefited only the rich section of the society, where the poor do not have access to such ventures.[83] She further clarified this point by interviewing two prominent sociologists[84] who assert that globalization has benefited a lot in terms of science and technology, but it has brought unwanted changes in the Khasi society affecting the traditional lifestyle and culture.[85] Furthermore, it has also encouraged a culture of consumerism and individualism and thus bringing in division among the rich and the poor and also posing a threat to the relationship and communitarian lifestyle of which the Khasi were famous for. Globalization and its related ideologies of urbanization and industrialization have resulted in mass migration of people from

---

[82] P.N. Dutta, *Impacts of the West on Khasi and Jaintias: A Survey of Political and Economic Change* (Delhi: Cosmo Publication, 1982), 202.

[83] Barbara Dohling, "Interrogating the Importance and Significance of *Tip Briew Tip Blei* (to know People is to know God) for Developing an Ethical Critique of the Contemporary Khasi Society" (Unpublished M.Th Thesis, Senate of Serampore College), 76.

[84] A.K. Nongkynrih and B. Lyngkhoi cited by Barbara Dohling, "Interrogating the Importance and Significance...," 76.

[85] *Ibid.*, 77.

remote areas to Shillong city for the sake of employment opportunities. This ultimately leads to over-population and increasing danger of environmental crisis. Thus, it can be inferred, that, globalization has brought the advancement in the field of technology at the same time it has affected the poor of the society, and marred the traditional cultural life styles of the Khasi.

Conclusion

From the above description of the Khasi society, we can draw the following conclusions: firstly, the Khasi society follows the matrilineal system, in which descent and lineage is traced from the mother's side. We can see that respective roles are given to men and women in the society and family affairs. Nevertheless, some changes have taken place in the present Khasi society due to the impact of westernization, modernization, urbanization and globalization on the socio-cultural milieu, whereby, many traditional moral, ethical values and norms are slowly diminishing. Secondly, the Khasi society being matrilineal in character is expected to have some space for women' participation, but what can be inferred from the above is otherwise. In the day to day transactions we can see the power of patriarchy operating in the system. Women are kept aloof from decision making process and other matters except the descent and lineage. This aspect probably needs an in depth research, which is beyond the scope of the present study. Nonetheless, the point to be made here is that patriarchy as an ideology has in some way or the other operated and continues to operate in the Khasi society. This ultimately leads to serious complications of which one of them is identified by the present research as domestic violence. The argument is that in most cases women are made targets of Domestic violence owing to the underlying notion of patriarchy. Apart from this, there are other related problems such as alcoholism, pornography, etc., which can also contribute to the emergence of the above problem. Therefore, the present research is an attempt to find out the possible linkages, dimensions and causes of the above problem in the Khasi society. Nevertheless, before entering into that aspect, we shall first emphasize on the theoretical and conceptual analysis of what domestic violence is all about.

Chapter 2

CONCEPTUALIZING AND CONTEXTUALIZING DOMESTIC VIOLENCE IN INDIA

Introduction

Domestic violence is a global issue today. It tops among the atrocities subjected on women across the world. The rate of violence in India alone is as high as 19 percent (coming after Zambia, which is leading in the world which reports a 48 percent violence rate) according to a survey released in New Delhi on the second day of the 34th Triennial congress of International Alliance of Women, hosted by the All India Women's Conference (AIWC) in association with International Alliance of Women (IAW) on 29lh October, 2007.[1] This chapter is an attempt to conceptualize and contextualize domestic violence in India. The objective is to analyze theoretically the possible forms or types of domestic violence, the possible factors causing it and the intensity with which it affects the Indian society. A note related to domestic violence and the legal mechanism will also be studied to add further clarity on the issue.

---

[1] "India second in atrocities on Women," *Legal News and Views* 21/12/ (December, 2007), 6-7, here 6.

2.1. Defining and Understanding Domestic Violence

According to the Chambers Concise Dictionary the word "Domestic" means belonging to a house, remaining much at home or private. On the other hand "Violence" connotes a state or quality of being violent, excessive, unrestrained or unjustifiable.[2] In wider form, violence can be defined as any act that results in, or is likely to result in, physical, sexual, or psychological harm or suffering to a person, including threats of such acts, coercion or arbitrary deprivation of liberty, whether occurring in public or private life.[3] Furthermore, it may also refer to one of the crucial social mechanism by which a person is forced into subordinate position compared to the other. It caused human to fear for the safety, distorts and limits a person's psyche and destroys his/her self confidence and sense of independence, dignity and humanity and even isolate one's physical, social or emotional being. Clubbing these two words together, "Domestic Violence" may refer to the form of violence present in the domestic set up or the violence that occur in the context of the family or house involving between the spouses or in some way or the other against the children or old aged. However, in both cases one is the victim and the other is the abuser, the powerful and the powerless.

Domestic violence can be described as when one adult in a relationship misuses power to control another. It is the establishment of control and fear in a relationship through violence and other forms of abuse. The violence may involve physical abuse, sexual assault and threats. Sometimes it is more subtle, like making someone feel worthless, not letting them have any money. Therefore, domestic violence refers to a range of behaviors from emotional to sexual abuse, to economic coercion, to acts of physical violence. Women are the vast majority of the victims of domestic violence, and it is one of the most serious human rights violation facing women globally. The term "Wife Battering" was previously used to refer to a series of abuses women face at home. Later on it was replaced

---

[2] G.W. Davidson, M.A. Seaton and J. Simpson, eds., *Chambers Concise 20th Century Dictionary* (New Delhi: Allied Publishers Ltd., 1991), 284 & 1114.

[3] Holly Johnson et.al., *Violence Against Women* (New York: Springer, 2008), 1.

by a more appropriate term "Domestic Violence."[4] Domestic violence can be understood not only in terms of physical harm but also as discrimination, deprivation, denial of access to resources, intimidation, exploitation, and other means whereby economic and social inequality is perpetuated-is a tool that reproduces the inherently hierarchical structure of the family.[5] Feminists have argued that domestic violence is tied up to gender roles in society; men in our society are trained to be more powerful, assertive, and in control, while women are trained to be passive, submissive and compliant and violence against women at home is one way that these gender roles are maintained. Indeed, for much of human history, women have been considered literally the property of their fathers, and then husbands, and domestic violence is simply one way that this ownership is demonstrated.[6] This ultimately leads to serious problems in the family where women are the majority of victims of

---

[4] Second wave feminists in the United States and England were the first to recognize violence against women in their homes as a problem and not simply one of the occupational hazards of being a woman. They coined the term "Wife Battering" to describe what they saw happening to many women, and they opened the first battered women's' shelters in the late 1960's so that abused women would have a safe place to escape the abuse. They also began broad challenges to the way that the legal and criminal justice systems address violence against women in the home. The term "Wife Battering" was later replaced by the broader term "Domestic Violence". Refer, Alison Piepmeier, "Domestic Violence," *The Women's Movement Today: An Encyclopedia of Third Wave Feminism,* edited by Leslie L. Heywood, vol. 1 (New Delhi: Rawat Publications, 2005), 96-97.

[5] Sobha Venkatesh Ghosh, "Contextualizing Domestic Violence: Family, Community, State," in *Behind Close Doors: Domestic Violence in India,* edited by Rinki Bhattacharya (New Delhi: Sage Publications, 2004), 57. Domestic Violence in some ways often becomes a tool to socialize family members according to prescribed norms of behavior within an overall perspective of male dominance and control. The family and its operational unit, the household, are the sites where oppression and deprivation of individual psyches and physical selves are a part of the structures of acquiescence; often enough, those being `moulded' into an acceptance of submission and denial are in-marrying women and children. Physical forms of aggression are used as methods to ensure obedience. Cf., Malavika Karlekar, "Breaking the Silence," in *Writing the Women's Movement: A Reader,* edited by Mala Khullar (New Delhi: Zubaan, 2005), 302-303.

[6] Cf., Alison Piepmeier, "Domestic Violence...," 97.

Domestic Violence. It has also to do as stated earlier more with the control and power that men exercise against women. It is a question of power and powerlessness that we see in the society and family. Therefore, Ghosh asserts that all violence within family is gendered.[7] The point here is that Patriarchy as an ideology has been employed to control and manipulate the victims, and Karlekar opines, "At every stage in the life, the female body is both the object of desire and control."[8] Domestic violence is therefore, the power, control and monopoly of which one person perpetuates on the other, through certain ways and means, in order to retain his/her position in the society or family.

2.2. Types/Forms of Domestic Violence

Domestic Violence is a social phenomenon; therefore, it was argued that there are no noticeable differences between the person who is battered and the one who is not. Moreover, this type of violence transgresses all the boundaries of caste, class, religion and is prevalent in almost all societies. The following are some of the most likely forms or types of violence that occur at a domestic level.

2.2.1. Physical Violence

Physical Violence ranges from pushing and shoving to slapping, hitting, stabbing, assault and murder.[9] In other words, it may also mean using hideous means that may lead to assault, serious injury or bums, in some cases it may be as grave as causing death to the victim. Chatterjee states that this of violence gets noticed because it is most obvious and the most visible form of violence,[10] where all the above ranges of violence can be seen explicitly.

---

[7] Sobha Venkatesh Ghosh, "Contextualizing Domestic Violence: Family, Community, State...," 57.

[8] Malavika Karlekar, "Breaking the Silence...," 303.

[9] Lise Lachance, *Marital Violence in Canada: A Journalistic Report* (Bombay: Research Centre for Women's Studies, 1994), 4.

[10] Shoma A. Chatterji, *Indian Women, from Darkness to Light* (Calcutta: Parumita Publications, 2000), 23.

2.2.2. Sexual Violence

Sexual Violence is defined as any form of non-consensual sexual activity, from unwanted sexual touching to rape. Lise Lachance writes, "Sexual Violence is the one that victims find the most difficult to admit, perhaps because it shakes the very foundation of manwoman relationships in a society where sexuality- even if it is taboo- defines the essence of male and female conditioning."[11] This type or form of violence has become very prominent in most families today. Marital rape[12] is the most common form of sexual violence women suffer. As rightly stated earlier it affects the marital relationship, therefore, even though it may be present, it may not be visible until and unless a victim reports it.

2.2.3. Psychological Violence

Psychological violence encompasses many tactics to undermine a person's self confidence such as taunts, jeers, shouting, insults, swearing, and abusive language, threats of physical violence or isolation.[13] This type or form of violence leads to deprivation of love and affection, concern, sympathy and care. In worse conditions, it

---

[11] Sexual violence may have a wider connotation and assume a psychological aspect; for instance if a man humiliates his wife comparing her to pin-ups in the magazines or if he obliges her to look at pornographic materials. Most of the violent partners are great consumers of pornography. Cf., Lise Lachance, *Marital Violence in Canada: A Journalistic Report...*, 4.

[12] Marital rape is rape of a wife by her husband and in many instances the act of rape is unequivocal. Marital rape rests primarily on the "sexualization of dominance and submission" within marriage. That is when the state and society mandates that the wife be sexually available to the husband; she becomes the property of the man. Cf., Rebecca Surtees, "Rape and sexual transgression in Cambodian society," in *Violence Against Women in Asian Societies,* edited by Lenore Manderson and Linda Rae Bennet (London: Routledge Curzon, 2003), 97. Marital rape is therefore, the unconsensual or force sexual intercourse, a partner impose on another partner, within the marital relationship.

[13] The deliberate withholding of various forms of emotional support may also be used. Some men resort to different emotional and psychological tactics to ensure that a woman cuts ties with her nuclear and extended families. These actions erode and eventually destroy a woman's social relationship, leaving her isolated and vulnerable. *Ibid.,* 4.

also includes depriving a person of the custody of children. This form of violence aims at attacking the psyche of a person, which will ultimately erode the social relationship leaving him/her isolated and vulnerable.

2.2.4. Financial Violence

Financial Violence or economic violence as Chatterjee puts it refers to the denial of assets to employment opportunities.[14] Lachance opines that "many a time one of the marital partner may deny the access to employment opportunities outside the home or to other avenues for gaining some financial independence such as part-time work or taking care of children at home. The violent partner withholds or maintains control over all substantial amounts of money.[15] This type of violence may also mean taking away the assets, which a person possesses or earns. Niroj Sinha is of the view that financial hardship coupled with responsibility and poverty preserve a violent relationship.[16] This goes on to show that that financial violence means not just denial of money but denial of opportunities which pushes a person to dependency. This ultimately is a mean to maintain control and power, leading to violence.

2.2.5. Verbal Violence

Verbal Violence means the use of abusive and filthy languages against the person or his/her near and dear ones. Madhurima opines that, "it includes shouting at each other and calling names. In case the arguments do not stop and quarrel persists, verbal violence is a natural consequence thereof."[17] It may be said that it is the dominant partner who in order to maintain their dominant position, resort to this form of violence.

---

[14] Shoma A. Chatterji, *Indian Women, from Darkness to Light...*, 25.

[15] Lise Lachance, *Marital Violence in Canada: A Journalistic Report...*, 5.

[16] Boa Niroj Sinha, "Profile of Marital Violence: Wife Battering," in *Women and Violence,* edited by Niroj Sinha (Delhi: Vikas Publishing House, 1989), 74.

[17] Madhurima, *Violence Against Women* (New Delhi: Gyan Publishing House, 1996), 70.

2.2.6. Intellectual Violence

This type or form of violence means a person must submit to the powerful member of the family. In most of the patriarchal societies, women are to be submissive to the will of men. In other words, women are looked upon as incapable and weak physically and intellectually, therefore, they are not allowed to take part in the decision making processes. The fact is in most Indian families for instance, wives should submit to the will of her husband. The issue here is the violent partner is looked as powerful whereas, the victim as vulnerable and weak.

All these forms of violence, which mainly occur at the family level or at a domestic set up, may differ from other forms of violence precisely because it does not appear suddenly, between strangers, but always in the frame of a privileged relation and because it includes the use of strength and threat.[18] It may be noted that the International Center for Research on Women (ICRW), an organization working on women's issues, stated that, in India alone 60 percent of married women regardless of caste, class and educational qualification experience some forms of violence in their homes. This reveals that half of married women in India are victims of Domestic Violence. Shiela Reddy asserts that for a few sensational cases, day-to-day abuses on women in their homes remain largely hidden.[19]

2.3. Factors Accelerating Domestic Violence

The factors which contributed towards the rise of domestic violence may be different from one society to the other, depending upon the social, moral cultural, economic and religious settings. In India, the following may perhaps be the possible factors that accelerate the rise of Domestic Violence.

2.3.1. Cultural Factor

When we talk of cultural factors and their relationship with violence, we cannot do away with the fact that violence is part of the culture,

---

[18] *Ibid.*, 5.

[19] Shiela Reddy, "Domestic Violence," *Women's Link 7/1* (January-March, 2001): 3-5, here 3.

element of day to day transactions in the society. The society legitimizes violence and this is reflected in the family violence or domestic violence to be precised. Conway quoted Baron and Strauss who write:

> The more the society tends to endorse the use of physical force to attain socially approved ends the greater is the likelihood that this legitimizes of force will be generalized to other spheres of life where force is less approved such as family and the relations between sexes.[20]

The violence is thus an outcome of one's culture. It is the culture that legitimizes violence whether in the society in general or family in particular. Turning to the Indian society, the lower status of women is legitimized by the culture, and this ultimately means women are vulnerable to intimidation and violence. Much of the violence inflicted on women is considered as natural part of male behavior and silently endured by women. This is looked upon as an outcome of patriarchy. It is all about retaining and maintaining power in the family. Menon and Johnson opine that "patriarchal control of women, especially within families, is virtually the prototypical type of paternalism, defined as a system under which an authority treats those under control in a fatherly way especially in regulating their conduct and supplying their needs."[21] Therefore, in a nutshell violence against women in the family is a product of the patriarchal culture of domination and control. Straus therefore asserts "cultural norms and sexual inequality are noted as causes of domestic violence."[22]

2.3.2. Psychological Factors

Domestic Violence may also have its origin in psychological factors like irrational and pathological behavior of the victim and the

---

[20] Helen L. Conway, *Domestic Violence and the Church* (Secunderabad: OM Books, 2003), 81.

[21] Niveditha Menon and Michael P. Johnson, "Patriarchy and Paternalism in Intimate Partner Violence: A Study of Domestic Violence in Rural India," in *Recent Studies on Indian Women,* edited by Kamal K. Misra and Janet Huber Lowry (New Delhi: Rawat Publications, 2007), 187.

[22] Cf., A. Strauss, "Wife Beating (1629-1934)," *Encyclopedia of Crime and Justice,* edited by Sanforn H. Karkirl (New York: Free Press, 1983): 1-10.

abuser, which subsequently affect the interpersonal relationship of both parties. This has been considered as the condition of 'learned helplessness'[23] Ghosh argued that in most cases of Domestic Violence, women do not feel that they are abused until they experience severe physical assault. This is because they have internalized the patriarchal norms of their family in particular and society in general.[24] Following the same line Chatterji opines that "a woman who has either seen or experienced violence as a child is likely to be more tolerant to different forms of violence than a woman who has been through a violence free childhood."[25] In such conditions Lachance argues "solving conflicts through violence seems acceptable to the victim."[26] Thus, this implies that victims of Domestic Violence endure violence or are silent owing to the reason of the psychological impact violence itself has on their lives. Another version of this is that a child who is himself/herself being abused by any adult member in the family becomes an aggressive and violent person in personal relationship, especially in relationship with the spouse. Chatterji further enunciate that there is this 'orthello syndrome', which is actually a morbid jealousy about his/her partner that makes a person

---

[23] Lise Lachance, *Marital Violence in Canada: A Journalistic Report...,* 14. According to 'learned helplessness' approach, some events occur in battered women's life during childhood and onwards with sufficient regularity. Because of this, they acquire feelings of helplessness and poor self-image and believe that they cannot escape abuse and that they only themselves are to be blamed. Some important events in women's lives which suggest a susceptibility factor include a high level of violence by members of their family in childhood, e.g., being battered by the mother, battered by the father, the father battering the mother, the father-mother battering other children, perception of critical or uncontrollable events in childhood, and experiencing such conditions which place them at high risk for depression. The fear of loosing husband's affection and the fear of disruption of home life status quo also prompts them to tolerate husband's battering. The battered wife is thus afraid to stay, and the same terrified to leave for fear of inescapable reprisals. Refer, Ram Ahuja, *Violence Against Women* (New Delhi: Rawat Publications, 2003), 174-175.

[24] Sobha Venkatesh Ghosh, "Contextualizing Domestic Violence...," 59.

[25] Cf., Chatterji, *Indian Women...,* 23.

[26] Lise Lachance, *Marital Violence in Canada: A Journalistic Report...,* 14.

reads imaginary meanings in the relationship with other people.[27] This attitude often leads to suspicion and ultimately may result in violent behavior. Chatterji quoted Elizabeth Wilson who asserts that "the psychological cause of male violence is the involvement of men to retain their power and authority in the family."[28] This factor undeniably is related to the wider connotations of power and inequality between sexes whether in the society or family. Most of the time as stated earlier Domestic Violence is related to the idea of control and monopoly of the women's psyche. In the Indian society precisely, men psychologically feel women should be controlled and this is legitimized by the existing socio- cultural and religious norms.

Apart from all these, another contributing psychological factor to Domestic Violence is fear. Fear of further violence pushes a person not to speak out of the violence one tolerated. The fear may be of the children in the family, or fear of increased possibility of aggression or even the fear that the aftermath of violence itself will bring dishonor to the family[29] and will never bring positive result.

2.3.3. Situational Factors

Situational factors are the problems, which the family concerned may face at any given time.[30] The situational factors may refer to the problem of poverty, alcoholism or drug addiction or even unemployment. Situational factors can be thought to be day to day occurrences in the family life, which cause the flash point at which violence occurs. In the Indian society, it is assumed that domestic

---

[27] Shoma A. Chatterji, *The Indian Women's Search for an Identity* (Delhi: Vikas Publishing House, 1989), 31.

[28] *Ibid.,* 27-28.

[29] The term "battered person" is a stigmatizing label that makes a person feel more powerless. Our society still calls marriage a success when people stay together for their lifetime even when they hate each other, as long as they hate each other privately. A person who is battered faces intense pressure not to tell. It is also a question of dignity. Person resist admitting their battering publicly because then they would have to open their wounds to the world: exposed or' naked, they would unable to preserve their dignity. Cf., Lachance, *Marital Violence in Canada: A Journalistic Report...,* 15.

[30] Helen L. Conway, *Domestic Violence and the Church...,* 81.

violence occur mostly in lower and middle class families, where poverty, unemployment or even alcoholism are quite common. However, the fact is that Domestic Violence cuts across economic, social and religious barriers.[31] Furthermore, Naroj Sinha reveals that despite economic independence women are subject to beating.[32] Apart, in most cases alcoholism is perceived to be one of the important causes of Domestic Violence,'[33] which is quite true to some extent. Nevertheless, the fact is that violence even occurs when the violent partner is sober.[34] It is therefore clear, that, the situational factors are significant causes of Domestic Violence, yet it cannot be ascertained that they are the only causes.

2.3.4. The Factors of Patriarchy, Status Inconsistency and Power Differentials

These factors are more to do with the domination of one partner over another. It can be concluded that only female are the target, nevertheless, looking generally, it can be argued that men are more aggressive than women. Male domination is enhanced by the use of power and status which is vested upon them through the nuances of patriarchy. The major factor behind male violent behavior as explicated by many researchers is the notion of patriarchy that operates in many societies. Sylvia Walby in her book, Theorizing

---

[31] Cf., Chatterji, *The Indian Women's Search...*, 29.

[32] Niroj Sinha "Profile of Marital Violence: Wife Battering...," 74.

[33] The account of the women about men who were violent when drunk focuses the blame for the violence on alcohol. These women feel that men are normal when sober, but become mean and violent like animals under the influence of liquor. Most of the women subscribe to the `conventional wisdom' that the alcohol affects people in such a way as to release pent-up frustrations. The assumption is that if men do not drink, they would not be violent. Refer, A. Mahajan, "Instigators of Wife Battering," in *Violence Against Women,* edited by Sushma Sood (Jaipur: Arihant Publishers, 1990), 6. Nevertheless, it is not very clear whether alcohol induces violent behavior directly or it acts as a disinhibitor of pre-existing aggressive tendencies. The latter hypothesis is perhaps supported that some perpetrators drink for courage prior to beating their wives (or committing crimes against persons). The use of alcohol in domestic violence may be accepted as a `cooperative factor" rather than the `basic' chief factor. Refer, Ram Ahuja, *Violence Against Women...*, 170.

[34] Chatterji, *The Indian Women's Search...*, 30.

Patriarchy calls it "a system of social structures and practices in which men dominate, oppress and exploit women."[35] Niroj Sinha opines that "patriarchy can be held as a strong reason and in communities where male dominance is strong; domestic violence is likely to be more frequent."[36] Turning to the Indian context women are perceived as mere object, to be used and manipulated by men. Therefore, patriarchy legitimizes violence on man-woman relationship. Dobash and Dobash are of the view that wife abuse is a form of behavior which has existed for centuries as an acceptable and, indeed, desirable part of a family system within patriarchal society.[37] Those who hold this view argue that our society is male dominated and that power is vested upon men to dominate and control women. All they say is that this is a man's world and so Domestic Violence is not surprising.

Status Inconsistency is another factor where status of male and female comes into play. Domestic Violence is born out of the frustration that occurs when the abuser feels his/her status within the family, as being lower than it should be. Most of the time the abuser is the male and the victim is the female. Chatterji enunciates that, "false superiority complex a man harbors about himself and the wife's own feeling of inferiority leads to Domestic Violence."[38] Furthermore, the important conditions which a man resorts to violence against women are status frustration, life stresses and career crisis.[39] The bottom line is that a person feels in-secured and gets frustrated when his/her status is lowered due to lower educational qualifications or lower jobs or even unemployment and therefore, opted to show his/her power through violence. The most likely to do so is the male owing to the already higher status conferred on him by society and religion. The male member feel the best place to show his supremacy is at home.

---

[35] Sylvia Walby, *Theorizing Patriarchy* (Oxford: Blackwell Publishers, 1990), 3.

[36] Niroj Sinha "Profile of Marital Violence: Wife Battering...," 68.

[37] Dobash and R.P. Dobash, "Wives: The Appropriate Victims of Domestic Violence," *Victimology*? 1314, (March-June 1978): 430-454, here 430.

[38] Chatterji, *The Indian Women's Search...,* 27.

[39] Dharam Vir and Kamlesh Mahajan eds., *Contemporary Indian Women,* vol. 2 (Delhi: Rawat Publications, 1996), 4-5.

The third factor is the power differentials or the exercise of power of a powerful on a less powerful. Power is a very important factor in a domestic violence. Filkenhor notes:

> The most common patterns are not just for the more powerful to abuse the less powerful, but for the most powerful to abuse the least. This is an interesting commonality. Abuse tends to gravitate to the relationship of greatest power differential.[40]

Lachance further argues, "Men are taught to be in control, a characteristic which is strongly valued by those who abuse their wives. Powerful people are seen as having power over others. This power may lead to psychologically violent behavior."[41] This is true also to the fact that when the abuser feels that his/ her power is lower outside the home but can keep great power in the home by the use of violence. This understanding is further enhanced in the Indian society by the already existing cultural, religious and social norms, which, look at women as least powerful. Therefore, a woman should be tolerant and receptive to what ever is given to her by her husband. It is a typical Indian mentality that a woman should be submissive, respecting her in laws and considering her husband as lord or master. In such a context, violence occurs when the woman is not going in tune with the set norms. It is therefore, "a tool of domination, an assertion of power, a gesture of control" opines Chatterji.[42] Power here, is used as a tool of the powerful to dominate and control the powerless. In the context of the family an abuser may use violence as a mean of power when he/she feels that his/her victim is gaining too much of power and wishes to put him/her back to his/her place. Power is used as legitimate authority,[43] where one seeks to dominate

---

[40] D. Filkenhor, et.al., *The Dark Side of Families* (London: Sage Publications, 1983), 117-118.

[41] Lachance, *Marital Violence in Canada: A Journalistic Report...,* 18.

[42] Cf., *Chatterji, Indian Women...,* 26.

[43] Malcolm Waters, *Modern Sociological Theory* (New Delhi: Sage Publications, 1998), 223-224. Max Weber through his theory called *Authoritative Theory* explains power in two ways: (i) authority as legitimate power and (ii) power exists when a person or group is able to extract compliance from other persons or groups, even in

the other, in many cases men have that authority to control on the basis of the existing cultural, social and religious norms.

2.3.5. Moral and Religious Factors

These factors refer to the legitimization of violence by the moral and religious teachings or principles. In every society the moral or religious teachings shaped the cultural, social and religious milieu of the people, they determine their social or religious behavior. Religion for that matter has been able in permeating discrimination based on sex in the family or society. Turning to the Indian society, we see the legitimization of violence against women through moral and religious teachings. For instance, Chatterji opines that Hindu texts subscribed by Manu gave guidance to men to beat up their wives. Tulsidas, the revert poet and saint went one step better on Manu and compared women with- `hold your breath- a drum, a rustic, an untouchable and an animal- adding that all of these are meant to be beaten.[44] Even Christianity is not far behind in this regard, classical theologians like Tertullian says, `women are the devil's gateway', while Thomas Aquinas opines that `woman is defective and misbegotten.'[45] These sayings and teachings arise out of the fact that the religious texts like the Bible is misinterpreted from the perspective of the male chauvinistic androcentric tendencies. Thus, moral and religious texts or teachings justify violence against women especially in the context of the family. The moral and religious customs, rituals and traditions in some way or the other seem to subjugate and suppress women's dignity and sanctity.

2.4. Domestic Violence: A Reality in India

Traditionally in all societies, the family is considered one of the most sacred places in the society. It is a source of comfort and nurturance

---

the face of opposition. The exercise of power in turn requires control of resources that are needed and desired by subordinates, and otherwise sufficiently available to them and or the ability to inflict harm on subordinates in the absence of a reciprocal ability.

[44] Cf., *Chatterji, Indian Women Search...*, 30.

[45] John T. Bristow, *What Paul Really Said About Women* (New York: Harper and Row, 1998), 1-29.

for the members. Nevertheless, the family is also not free from problems. All marital problems are happening between the two individuals, i.e., the husband and wife who constitute an important part of a family apart from other members. But when it comes to violence, who is more aggressive between the two, the husband or wife, man or woman? Does the sex of the individual have anything to do with being aggressive or violent? The answer is yes, one of the sexual partners is bound to be aggressive and violent in a marital relationship. Turning to Indian society since it follows a patriarchal system; therefore, women are mainly targeted and dominated by male member in the family. Let us see this in the following paragraphs. The fact that domestic violence is a global problem was brought out in the public through a UN Report published in November 30, 1989. For the first time ever, violence against women within the home became officially acknowledged part of the UN agenda. Chatterji quoted Jane Connors who authored the UN Report said, "It is a popular misconception that the home is a place of safety. Violence against women in the street does occur but the most likely place for it to happen is in the home. The person most likely to perpetrate for it is the husband."[46] Turning to the Indian situation domestic violence is a very serious issue. According to UN statistics, a woman is assaulted every five minutes in India. According to provisional figures for 2004 compiled by the National Crimes Record Bureau 142035 crimes against women is recorded in 2004. About 132 abused every day by the husband or in-laws in the year, i.e., 5 abused every hour, 18 dowry deaths every day and 1 dowry death every 80 minutes.[47] Still further according to the National Crimes Record Bureau report 2005, 1 crime is committed against women every 3 minutes, 1 case of cruelty on women by husband and relatives is reported every 9 minutes and 1 dowry death case occurs every 77 minutes.[48] The figure above shows that crimes against women, particularly at home

---

[46] Cf., Shoma A. Chatterji, *Indian Women…*, 26.

[47] Shanta B. Astige, "The Protection of Women from Domestic Violence Act, 2005: Its relevance to the present Indian society," *Legal News and Views* 21/10 (October 2007), 11-14, here 11.

[48] Shalu Nigam, "Law on Domestic Violence: An Urgent Need to Break Silence," *Legal News and Views* 20/12 (December 2006): 4-5, here 4.

is really a growing concern for everyone. In fact the overall percentage of domestic violence in India is as high as 37.2%, affecting 30.4% of urban women and 40.2% of rural women, according to the National Family and Health Survey-3 (NFHS-3) conducted by the Union Ministry of Health and Family Welfare.[49] Thus, it is clear from the above statistics that women across castes, class or locations have been victims of domestic violence in India.

In India as stated earlier, the most common form of family violence is related to dowry cases. As per statistics, every year in India, 5000 brides are murdered or force to commit suicide because their dowry is inadequate. The National Crimes Record Bureau reveals a shocking 75.5% increase in cases of torture and dowry deaths from 1991-2001 and there were about 1.5 lakh cases of domestic violence till 2003.[50] All of these figures are based on official records. It can be inferred that the actuality would be far greater, where many cases of domestic violence go unreported. Moreover, the information has been recorded sometimes back and probably the numbers of cases are on the rise as time go by. Violence especially in the marital relationship manifests itself in different forms and degrees, from cases of physical violence, which may lead even to the death of the victim, to more subtle and pervasive forms of violence. Domestic violence is today an important issue in the Indian society, which needs concrete and urgent response.

2.5. The Law and Domestic Violence in India

International conventions, the constitution and various legal provisions provide certain rights and protection to women against domestic violence. Nevertheless it comes as a surprise to know that only 44 countries have laws against domestic violence. Only 17 countries have made marital rape a criminal offence and only 27 countries have passed laws on sexual harassment. In India some of the important legal dimensions related to domestic violence are the

---

[49] Domestic Violence Rises in India," *Legal News and Views 21/4* (April, 2007): 13-14, here 14.

[50] Mary Scaria, "Domestic Violence Act: Will women be safe Now?," *Legal News and Views 19/10* (December 2005): 4-6, here 4.

provisions in the Indian Penal code (IPC) like the section 498A, which deal with cruelty in matrimonial relationship or section 304B which deals with dowry deaths. Recently, the Protection of Women from Domestic Violence Act, 2005 is enacted to deal with the problem of domestic violence. The following paragraphs attempt to study these legal provisions which are important for further clarity on the issue.

2.5.1. IPC-Section 498A and Section 304B

Before the year 1983 there was no specific legal provision pertaining to violence against women at domestic front. Therefore an amendment was made in 1983, which added section 498A to chapter XVI, IPC.[51] With the introduction of Section 498A, in the Indian Penal Code it was assumed that the legal instrument has been enacted to end dowry and related violence. The section 498A defines cruelty as `any willful conduct which is of such nature as is likely to derive the woman to commit suicide or cause grave injury or danger to life, or health (whether mental or physical) of the woman; or harassment of the woman where such harassment is with a view to coercing her or any person related to her to meet with any unlawful demand for any property or valuable security. The punishment for cruelty against wife is imprisonment for a term that may extend to three years and shall be liable to fine.'[52] Section 304B stipulates punishment for the crime of dowry death.[53] It is through the introduction of these sections (498A and 304B) to Indian Penal Code that the criminal behavior of husband is made punishable. However, Shalu Nigam asserts that "experiences over the years reveal that these sections though significant, are not sufficient.[54] Therefore, it is necessary to

---

[51] Shalu Nigam, *Understanding Justice Delivery System from Perspective of Women Litigants as Victims of Domestic Violence in India, Specially in the Context of Section 498A, IPC* (New Delhi: Centre for Women's Development Studies, 2005), 4.

[52] Seema Durrany, "Legal Responses to Domestic Violence in India," *Legal News and Views 19/10* (November 2005):4-6, here 4.

[53] Sections 3 and *4* of the Dowry Prohibition Act, *1961* and section *406* of Indian Penal Code for criminal breach of trust are also made applicable to marital dispute where cruelty is involved. *Ibid.*, 4.

[54] Shalu Nigam, "Law on Domestic Violence...," 4.

enact a law, keeping the rights guaranteed in article 15[55] of the Indian constitution. Accordingly, the Protection of Women from Domestic Violence Act, 2005 came into being to strengthen the existing laws on domestic violence.

2.5.2. The Protection of Women from Domestic Violence Act, 2005

The protection of women from Domestic Violence Act, 2005 is a golden piece of legislation, which came into force on 26th October 2006. This Act mandates, "an Act to provide for more effective of the rights of women guaranteed under the Constitution who are victims of violence of any kind occurring within the families and for matter connected therewith or incidental thereto."[56] Furthermore, this Act covers those women who are or have been in a relationship with the abuser where both parties have lived together in a shared household and are related by consanguinity, marriage or through a relationship in the nature of marriage or adoption.[57] All these categories of relationships are entitled for protection under this legislation. Apart, the definition of `domestic violence' has been extended to include actual abuse or threat or abuse that is physical, sexual, verbal, emotional or economic. Harassment by way of unlawful dowry demands to the women or her relatives would also be covered under this definition.[58] Authorized Officers under this Act are police officer, protection officer, service provider and the magistrate.[59] Aggrieved person or a Protection Officer or any other person may present an application to the magistrate seeking one or more reliefs under this Act.[60] An aggrieved person can ask

---

[55] Equality of sexes is enshrined in the Indian constitution as a fundamental right and no one should discriminate any body on the grounds of religion, caste, sex or place of birth.

[56] Shalu Nigam, "Law on Domestic Violence...," 4.

[57] Seema Durrany, "Legal Responses to Domestic Violence in India...," 4.

[58] Jose Kurian, "Protection of Women from Domestic Violence," *Legal' News and Views 20/1* (January 2006): 8-9, here 8.

[59] Jessy Kurian, "Some Aspects of the Protection of Women from Domestic Violence Act, *2005," Legal News and Views 22/1* (January- June 2008): 7-8, here 7.

[60] Ibid., 8.

from the court the reliefs under this Act such as to reside in a shared household, Protection orders, Residence orders, Monetary reliefs, Custody orders and Compensation orders.[61]

---

[61] Right to Reside in a Shared Household:

According to the Act every woman in a domestic relationship shall have the right to reside in a shared household, whether or not she has any right, title or beneficial interest in the same.

Protection Orders:

If the magistrate is satisfied that domestic violence has taken place or likely to take place, the magistrate passes a protection order in favor of the aggrieved person and prohibit the respondent from: I.

1. Committing any act of domestic violence.
2. Aiding or abetting in the commission of acts of domestic violence.
3. Entering the place of employment of the aggrieved person or, if the person aggrieved is a child, the school or any other place frequented by the aggrieved person.
4. Attempting to communicate in any form, whatsoever with the aggrieved person including personal oral or written or electronic or telephonic contact.
5. Alienating any assets, operating bank lockers or bank accounts, used or held or enjoyed by both the parties, jointly by the aggrieved person and the respondent or singly by the respondent.
6. Causing violence to the dependants, other relatives or any person who give the aggrieved person assistance from domestic violence.
7. Committing any other act as specified in the protection order.

Residence Orders:

The magistrate having been satisfied that domestic violence has taken place shall pass the following orders:

1. Restraining the respondent from disposing or in any other manner disturbing the possession of the aggrieved person from the shared household.
2. Directing the respondent to remove himself from the shared household.
3. Restraining the respondent or any of his relatives from entering any portion of the shared household in which the aggrieved person resides.
4. Restraining the respondent from alienating or disposing of the shared household.
5. Restraining the respondent from renouncing his rights in the shared household, except with the permission of the magistrate.

Monetary Relief:

An aggrieved person can seek monetary relief for the following:

1. Loss of earnings
2. Medical expenses

Conclusion

Domestic violence as we have seen is a global issue today, particularly in the Indian society which is marred by problems like dowry and other forms of discrimination against women. It can be argued that the notion of patriarchy and its related ideologies help legitimizing and perpetrating violence against women especially at the domestic front. The intensity and forms of domestic violence range from physical, verbal psychological and economical. Apart from this, domestic violence is caused and legitimized through certain factors like cultural, moral, religious, status differential and patriarchy. We have seen that domestic violence is indeed a major issue today not just concerning women folk alone but disturbing the whole fabric of the Indian society. Therefore, violence in any form or dimension needs to be confronted and tackled. The existing legal measures are indeed a benefit to the victims, yet it can be argued that the cases of domestic violence are on the rise. The interesting point is that domestic violence is a fact across societies, castes, languages and occupations. Thus, it is imperative that an urgent constructive and responsible action has to be taken to challenge the rise of domestic violence in the world and India particularly. The next chapter devotes itself in analyzing the dimensions and factors of the prevalence of domestic violence in the Khasi Matrilineal society, which otherwise is thought that this problem is not relevant since women are enjoying better facilities and status than their counter parts in patriarchal societies.

---

3. Loss caused due to destruction, damage or removal of any property from the control of the aggrieved person
4. Maintenance of the aggrieved person as well as her children. Cf., *Ka Jinglam khmat Kyllum jong ki Lawyers Collective Halor ka Hok jong ki Kynthei* (Shillong: North East Network, n.d.), 2-15. See also, Jessy Kurian, "Some Aspects of the Protection of Women from Domestic Violence Act, 2005...," 7-8.

Chapter 3

ANALYZING DOMESTIC VIOLENCE IN THE KHASI MATRILINEAL SOCIETY

Introduction

In the previous chapter we have learnt that domestic violence is a global problem crossing across barriers of caste, class, gender, languages and qualifications. No society is free from domestic violence. We have also noted the fact that it is an issue of concern in the Indian society. This is premised on a fact that Indian society is a patriarchal society; therefore, domestic violence especially against women is very common. Nevertheless, as stated above this is not just a phenomenon of the patriarchal society alone, it can also be an issue in the Matrilineal society. This chapter devotes itself in analyzing this issue pertaining to the Khasi matrilineal society. The argument is that superficially matrilineal society seems not to have domestic violence against women as they are thought to enjoy more rights and privileges than their counterparts in other societies in the world. Nonetheless, the fact is that domestic violence is a malady in the present Khasi society. Therefore, this venture is carried on to prove that women are victims of domestic violence in the Khasi matrilineal society. On the other hand, the point to be noted is the possibility that in matrilineal society men are also victims of domestic violence.

This study is conducted by collecting and analyzing the data and views through questionnaires and interviews, which will aid in revealing the above proposition.

3.1. Sample

The sample emphasizes on two aspects, firstly, the general description of the sample area selected for the study with the number of respondents and the name of each village or locality as shown in table no. A. Secondly, the detailed description of respondents is shown in table nos. B.I., B.II. , B.111., and B.IV.

3.1.1. General Description

The sample area selected for the research includes seven different localities in Shillong city and two other villages, namely Sohra and Mawsynram. Shillong is the capital of Meghalaya, one of the North Eastern States of India. Shillong as of the 2001 census has an approximate population of 232,946. Males constitute 49% and females 51% of the total population. Shillong has a literacy rate of over 80%.[1] Geographically the city is divided into different localities. Approximately there are 35 localities. It has a mixed population comprising of people from different parts of North East India, and a significant numbers of Bengalis, Nepalis, Biharis and others. Nevertheless, the Khasis who are the local inhabitants are the majority.

On the other hand, Sohra and Mawsynram are the villages in the East Khasi Hills District of Meghalaya, both approximately 50-60 kilometers away from Shillong city, and dominated by the Khasi population. Sohra previously known as Cherrapunjee is a village with an estimated population of 10,086. It has a literacy rate of approximately 74%. Furthermore, Mawsynram is a village 16 kilometers west of Sohra with an estimated population of 9030 and a literacy rate of about 53%. The sample therefore, is a crosssection of people in the Khasi Matrilineal Society. The following table indicates the names of localities/villages surveyed and the number of respondents in each locality/villages.

---

[1] "Shillong," http:// en.wikipedia.org/wiki/Shillong (28 Jan 2010).

Table No. A. Names of Localities/Villages Studied and Number of Respondents Localities/Villages-wise

SI.No	Name of Locality/Village	Number	Percentage
1	Nongthymmai	15	20.0
2	Mawlai	10	13.3
3	Malki	9	12.0
4	Mawkhar	8	10.6
5	Laitumkhrah	8	10.6
6	Wahingdoh	6	8.0
7	Laban	7	9.3
8	Mawsynram	6	8.0
9	Sohra	6	8.0
	Total	75	100.0

The above table shows that the respondents are from the different localities'[2] in Shillong city, where the bulk of the study is concentrated. The table points out that more than two thirds of the respondents (Serial Nos 1, 2, 3, 4, 5, 6&7) to be precise 84% of the respondents belong to different localities in Shillong. There are two villages, Mawsynram and Sohra which fall outside the city of Shillong, which are also used in the sample for a wider perspective on the study. However, they constitute only 16% of the total number of respondents. Among the localities Nongthymmai has the highest number of respondents and Wahingdoh has the least number. The villages of Mawsynram and Sohra have only 6 respondents each.

---

[2] Locality represents an area with a specific boundary and population. Each of them has *a Rangbah **Shnong*** (Head man) who looks after the welfare and well-being of each locality. The locality has a local council called *Durbar* which is headed by the *Rangbah Shnong* and has its own of governance and policies for the benefit and development of the locality as a whole. The number of localities formed the city of Shillong.

3.1.2. Respondents

There are 75 respondents representing men and women from different localities/villages, qualifications, marital statuses and age groups. The detailed description is given below:

3.1.2.1. Respondents-Gender wise

The table below represents the respondents-gender wise. There are 37 male and 38 female respondents.

Table No. B. I. Respondents-Gender-wise

Gender	Number	Percentage
Male	37	49.3
Female	38	50.7
Total	75	100.0

The above table indicates that 49.3% of the respondents are male and 50.7% are female. This shows that the total male and female respondents are almost equal in number. This will definitely have important bearing on the findings of the study as it helps to get an inclusive view.

3.1.2.2. Respondents-Qualification-wise

The respondents belong to different qualifications ranging from under matric, secondary/higher secondary, graduate, post graduate and above post graduate categories. The respondents-qualification wise is given in Table no. B.II below:

Table No. B. II. Respondents-Qualification-wise

Qualification	Number	Percentage
Under Matric	03	4.0
Secondary/Higher Secondary	10	13.3
Graduation	36	48.0
Post-Graduation	25	33.3
Above Post Graduation	01	1.3
Total	75	100.0

The above table shows that almost half of the respondents i.e., 48% are graduates. Apart 33.3% are post-graduates. This demonstrates that the study bears a relatively higher amount of respondents belonging to the graduate and post-graduate categories. The table also reveals that only 13.3% of the respondents belong to the secondary or higher secondary group, 4% of them under matric and only 1.3% are above post graduate level.

3.1.2.3. Respondents-Marital Status-wise

The respondents according to their marital statuses are divided into three categories, namely, married, unmarried and widow. This is shown in the table below:

Table No. B. III. Respondents-Marital Status-wise

Marital Status	Number	Percentage
Married	36	48.0
Unmarried	37	49.3
Widow	02	2.6
Total	75	100.0

The above table specifies that 48% of the respondents are married. Furthermore, 49.3% are unmarried and 2.6% are widow. These figures reflect the fact that almost equal numbers of respondents are either married or unmarried. This will help to have a comprehensive consensus when the data are tabulated and analyzed. Furthermore, only 2.6% are widows, which mean their husbands have passed away. There are no divorcees found in the study conducted.

3.1.2.4. Respondents-Age wise

The respondents are divided into three age groups, namely, 18-35 years, 36-50 years and 51-75 years respectively. However, the overwhelming majority of the respondents belong to the age group of 18-50 years. This is shown in the table below:

Table No. B. IV. Respondents Age wise

Age	Number	Percentage
18-35 years	31	41..3
36-50 years	24	32.0
51-75 years	20	26.7
Total	75	100.0

The above table above points out that the age group ranges from 18 to 75 years. About 41.3% of the respondents fall within the age group between 18 to 35 years of age. Furthermore, 32% of the respondents belong to the age group between 36 to 50 years of age and 26.7% of them are within the age group between 51 to 75 years. The above table indicates that an overwhelming majority i.e. 73.3% of the respondents are within the category of 18 to 50 years of age. This signifies that this study concentrates more on the younger and middle age group components. The number of respondents belonging to age group between 51 to 75 years of age is 26.7% which is only one thirds of the total respondents.

3.2. Awareness of Domestic Violence

The table below depicts the awareness of the people about domestic violence in their own localities or villages.

Table No. C. I. Awareness of Domestic Violence

Gender	Yes	No
Male	37	0
Female	38	0
Total	75	0
Percentage	100.0	0.0

Table no. C.I reveals the fact that all i.e., 100% the respondents comprising of both male and female agree that they are aware about domestic violence in their localities or villages. This goes on to show that this issue is very important in the Khasi matrilineal society.

3.3. Sources from where Domestic Violence is Learnt About

There are different sources from where people learnt or heard about domestic violence in their respective localities or villages. The following table exposes these sources.

Table No. C. II. Sources from where Domestic violence is learnt about

Gender	Newspapers		Television		School / College		Church	
	Yes	No	Yes	No	Yes	No	Yes	No
Male	31	6	22	15	9	28	5	32
Female	33	5	24	14	3	35	2	36
Total	64	11	46	29	12	63	7	68
Percentage	85.3	14.7	61.3	38.7	16.0	84.0	9.3	90.7

Table no. C.II. shows 85.3 % of the respondents learnt about Domestic Violence from the newspaper and 61.3% from television which shows that media awareness plays a very important role in this regard. On the contrary only 16% of the respondents opine that they have learnt or heard about the issue from School/College or other places of learning. Only about 9.3% of the respondents agree that they have learnt about the issue from the Church. These figures show that Domestic Violence is not an area of concern in the Schools/ Colleges or any other places of learning and even in the Church. Still further, few came to know about Domestic Violence through their neighbors and friends in their respective localities/villages.[3]

3.4. Prevalence of Domestic Violence

The table below shows the prevalence of domestic violence in each locality or village.

[3] Interview with B. Laloo, Headman Lawjynriew, Shillong, 12 September, 2009.

Table No. D. Prevalence of Domestic Violence

Gender	Yes	No
Male	32	5
Female	34	4
Total	66	9
Percentage	88.0	12.0

From the above table 88% of the respondents comprising of both males and females agree that cases of domestic violence is prevalent in their localities/villages. This shows that the Khasi Matrilineal society is facing domestic violence. Patricia Mukhim is of the opinion that even though cases are rampant, they still remain a hidden issue owing to many reasons, one of them being that it is most of the time taken to be a personal matter not to be publicized.[4] D.S. Mawlong asserts that reporting is considered as a social stigma therefore cases of violence are not revealed or reported.[5] Nevertheless, Theilin Phanbuh opines that today the issue is more open and women are speaking out mainly due to sensitization programs conducted by various state agencies, NGO's etc. further, she states that approximately from 2016-2018 more 100 cases are reported to the State Women Commission.[6] However, the National Family Health Survey reports that only 12% of women who have experienced physical or sexual violence have sought help. Almost 74% of women neither sought help nor told anyone about the violence.[7] The above table proves that domestic violence is a reality in the present Khasi society.

[4] Interview with Patricia Mukhim, Padmashree Awardee, Shillong, 9 January, 2010. (Here after cited as Interview with Patricia Mukhim).

[5] Interview with D.S. Mawlong, Headman, Kenches Trace, Oxford and Rilbong, Shillong, 12 September, 2009. (Here after cited as Interview with D.S. Mawlong).

[6] Interview with Theilin Phanbuh, Chairperson, Meghalaya State Commission for Women, Shillong, 6 March, 2019.

[7] National Family Health Survey 2015-2016, Meghalaya, http://www.meghalaya.pdf.rchilps.org>nfhs, accessed on 6 March, 2019.

3.5. Women and Domestic Violence

Anywhere in the globe as we have learnt from the previous chapter women are the main victims of domestic violence. Nevertheless, can we consider that this is true to Khasi matrilineal society? This is a question that is most of the time ruled out owing to the supposition that there is no violence against women in matrilineal society as they enjoy better privileges than men. Therefore, the following paragraphs will attempt to give an answer to this question.

3.5.1. Women as main targets of Domestic Violence

The table below shows that women are the main targets of domestic violence in each locality or village.

Table No. E. I. Women as main targets of Domestic Violence

Marital status	Yes	No
Married	24	12
Unmarried	27	10
Widow	2	0
Total	53	22
Percentage	70.7	29.3

The above table shows that an overwhelming majority of 70.7% of the respondents which comprise of 24 married, 27 unmarried and 2 widows, agree that women are the main targets of domestic violence in their locality/village. This does away the assumption that there is no domestic violence against women in the Khasi matrilineal society. L Dkhar reveals the fact that in the Police Case Report kept in the Medical Report Department of the Civil Hospital, Shillong; there are 31 cases of Domestic Violence in 2008 alone of which 13 are cases of burn injuries and 20 of alleged assault being reported. In 2009 till the month of August, 15 cases of burn injuries and 9 cases of alleged assault are recorded. Most of the victims are women in the age group of 18 to 35.[8] The above table also discloses that only 29.3%

[8] Interview with I. Dkhar, Medical Report Technician, Civil Hospital Shillong, 14 September, 2012.

which only one thirds of the respondents think that women are not victims of domestic violence. Darilin Syiem argues that the highest of cases were reported from East Khasi Hills District with 117 cases out of 133 reported in other districts of Jaintia Hills, West Khasi Hills and Ri Bhoi. She further said out of 133 cases, 108 are from tribal women and only 25 cases are from non-tribal women. This is an indicator that all is not well in the Khasi Matrilineal Society.[9] However, the National Family Health Survey reports that in 2015-2016 the rate of domestic violence is 28.7% as compared to 12.8% in 2005-2006. Furthermore, the survey also reports that women aged between 15-49, 27% have experienced violence.[10] Therefore, the above data reveals that women are the main targets of domestic violence in the Khasi Matrilineal society.

3.5.2. Types of Domestic Violence Women suffer

Women suffer different types or forms of domestic violence ranging from physical, verbal, sexual and emotional in the Khasi matrilineal society. The table below exposes this aspect.

Table No. E. II. Types of Domestic Violence Women suffer

Marital status	Physical		Verbal		Sexual		Emotional	
	Yes	No	Yes	No	Yes	No	Yes	No
Married	30	6	21	15	21	15	24	12
Unmarried	29	8	21	16	23	14	25	12
Widow	2	0	1	1	2	0	1	1
Total	61	14	43	32	46	29	50	25
Percentage	81.3	18.7	57.3	42.7	61.3	38.7	66.7	33.3

Table no. E.11. gives the picture of the different forms of Domestic Violence women sufferin the Khasi Matrilineal Society. The most common type of Domestic Violence women undergo is

[9] "Matrilineal Society also tops in Domestic Violence", http://wwww.shillongtimes.com, December 16 2014, accessed on 16 October, 2018.

[10] National Family Health Survey, http://www.oxfamindia.org>2018. Accessed on 6 March, 2019.

Physical Violence. About 81.3% of the respondents comprising of both married and unmarried men and women including the widows agree that Physical violence is a very common type of domestic violence in their locality/village. Furthermore, K. Prasad claims that out of three cases reported to the Police under the Prevention of Domestic Violence Act, 2005 all were Physical in nature.[11] The above table also gives an idea that women also suffer Sexual violence of which 61.3% of the respondents consider so. This is very common type of violence women suffer these days in the form of marital rape of which Pornography do play a vital role in aggravating this form of violence (this will be dealt in the other section). Around 29% of women have experienced spousal physical or sexual violence from their husbands.[12] Again about 57.3% of the respondents are of the view that women also suffer verbal abuse in their homes from their husbands. About 66.7% of the respondents also opine that women also suffer emotional form of violence. The above table, therefore, shows that women suffer all the four forms of domestic violence. The study also reveals that these forms are connected to one another, where emotional violence is the outcome of physical violence or verbal abuse. Sexual violence may result in physical violence.

3.6. Causes of Domestic Violence

As we have discussed in the previous chapter, there are numerous factors which cause domestic violence (detailed discussion in Chapter Two, sub section 2.3.). In the following tables we will be focusing on some of the important factors which are considered to be the main causes of domestic violence in the Khasi matrilineal society.

3.6.1. Situational and Psychological Factors

The table below shows the situational and psychological factors. These are thought to be one of the main causes of domestic violence.

---

[11] Interview with K. Parasad, Office in charge, Sadar Police Station, Shillong, 15 September, 2009.

[12] National Family Health Survey 2015-2016, Meghalaya, http://www.meghalaya.pdf.rchilps.org>nfhs, accessed on 6 March, 2019.

Table No. F. I. Situational and Psychological Factors

Gender	Alcoholism			Poverty/ Unemployment	Extra Marital	Affairs
	Yes	No	Yes	No	Yes	No
Male	33	4	22	14	25	12
Female	36	2	21	18	22	16
Total	69	6	43	32	47	28
Percentage	92.0	8.0	57.3	42.7	62.6	37.4

Alcoholism, Extra-marital affairs and Unemployment/Poverty fall under what is termed as situational and psychological factors. The above table shows that an overwhelming majority i.e. 92% of the respondents agree that Alcoholism is the main contributing factor towards domestic violence in the Khasi society. It is actually a traditional but simplistic view that all domestic violence is caused by abusers under the influence of alcohol. A simple fact here is that men are the abusers and women are the victims. The account of women about men who were violent when drunk focuses the blame for the violence on alcohol. These women feel that men are normal when sober, but become mean and violent under the influence of liquor. Most of the women subscribe to the 'conventional wisdom' that the alcohol affects people in such a way as to release pent-up frustrations. The assumption is that if men do not drink, they would not be violent.[13] Men use alcohol as a mean to become violent in the marital relationship. Rica Lamar speaking on this asserts that more cases of domestic violence is reported in the families where one of the partners (usually a male member) is an alcoholic.[14] Patricia Mukhim opines that alcohol actually provokes a male member or acts as an igniter to make them more aggressive in the marital relationship. She goes on to say that most men are either feeling in secured or either abused in their work place and that frustration is shown on the helpless people in the family especially wife and children. In order

[13] Refer, A. Mahajan, "Instigators of Wife Battering...," 6

[14] Interview with Rica Lamar, Vice Chairperson, Meghalaya State Women Commission, 16 September, 2009. (Here after cited as Interview with Rica Lamar).

to do this alcohol is taken as a mean to create a violent situation[15] it is a 'co-operative factor' in this sense.[16] On the other hand, it cannot be taken for granted that only alcoholics are violent; the study found out few cases of domestic violence which occur without the influence of alcohol. Alcoholism cannot be projected as the only reason for the violent behavior of most men in the family. On the contrary, violence has to do more with the psychology of domination and control men have on women in the society and family. Alcohol only aids in maintaining the superior attitude men has against women using violence as a way to express that mindset.

Furthermore, 56% of the respondents believe that Extra-marital affairs of either partner may be the cause of domestic violence. Often one of the partner becomes suspicious of the movements of the other which may lead to verbal abuse and finally to physical violence. This psychologically affects the relationship. It was reported by Rica Lamar that in one of the cases she encountered that a husband became very violent just because his wife is seen talking to other men.[17] The feeling of suspicion can therefore leads to extreme cases of domestic violence. Suspicion of one of the partner on the other of having extra- marital affairs is the cause of domestic violence in the present Khasi society. Suspicion may be categorized as psychological factor as it is more related to the psyche of a person. It is the psychological effect of suspicion that leads to domestic violence.

Furthermore, another important factor which is considered as one of the causes of domestic violence in the Khasi society is unemployment which ultimately results in poverty. About 57.3 percent of the respondents believe that unemployment/poverty leads to domestic violence. Unemployment and poverty are intertwined, as unemployment may be the cause of poverty. Therefore, sometime they may bring about frustration and misunderstanding in the family resulting in domestic violence. However, this cannot taken for granted to be the only reason for violence as there are numerous cases where family violence is a happening in rich and well to do families

---

[15] Interview with Patricia Mukhim.

[16] Refer, Ram Ahuja, *Violence Against Women...,* 170.

[17] Interview with Rica Lamar.

also. Nevertheless, unemployment/poverty contributes to the rise of domestic violence in the Khasi society.

3.6.2. The factor of Pornography

Pornography is one of the factors perpetuating domestic violence against women in the Khasi matrilineal society. The table below explains this dimension.

Table No. F. II. Pornography as a factor perpetuating Domestic Violence

Qualification	Yes	No
Under Matric	3	0
Secondary/Higher Secondary	7	3
Graduate	28	8
Post Graduate	17	8
Above Post Graduate	1	0
Total	56	**19**
Percentage	74.7	25.3

Pornography also has a link with domestic violence in the Khasi society. Almost one thirds of the respondents i.e. 74.7% believe that pornography is one of the causes of domestic violence. Even though the larger numbers of respondents agree, yet it cannot be generalized. Patricia Mukhim believes that pornography is the issue of the educated section of the people who therefore have access to the internet and other facilities. However, the rest of the population especially in the villages does not have easy availability to pornography.[18] The above table also reveals that the graduates and post graduates comprise about 80.3% of the total respondents who believe that pornography is a cause of domestic violence, which therefore authenticate the above view. The question now arise which type of domestic violence is associated with pornography? The table below will answer this question.

[18] Interview with Patricia Mukhim.

3.6.2.1. The type/form of Domestic Violence associated with Pornography

The following table no. F.III. reveals the different forms of domestic violence associated with pornography.

Table No. F. III. The Types of Domestic Violence associated with Pornography

Qualification	Sexual		Emotional		Physical	
	Yes	No	Yes	No	Yes	No
Under Matric	3	0	1	2	2	1
Secondary/Higher Secondary	7	3	5	5,	5	5
Graduate	25	11	15	21	21	15
Post Graduate	16	9	9	16	16	9
Above Post Graduate	1	0	1	0	0	1
Total	52	23	28	47	44	31
Percentage	69.3	30.7	37.3	62.7	58.7	41.3

Majority of the respondents i.e. 69.3% of them agree that pornography leads to sexual violence. Sexual violence here is associated to marital rape. Men who learn about sex through watching pornography, then, will treat women as existing solely for their sexual desires, and will not hesitate to assault women and force sex on them.[19] Actually after viewing some porn sites or movies and sometime under or even without the influence of alcohol a man becomes very demanding sexually and if these demands are not met he tends to become very aggressive. This may result in marital rape or even physical violence where bashing and shoving take place. Almost two thirds i.e. 58.7% of the respondents agree that Pornography also lead to severe physical violence.

[19] Jennifer Mather Saul, *Feminism: Issues and Arguments* (New York: Oxford University Press, 2003), 81. For a Christian response on pornography see, Shivraj Kumar Mahendra, *A Christian Response to Pornography* (Delhi: ISPCK, 2007).

3.6.3. Shift from Joint to Nuclear Family System as a Factor

The shift from joint to nuclear family system is one of the factors causing domestic violence in the Khasi matrilineal society. The table below elucidates this aspect.

Table No. F. IV. Shift from Joint to Nuclear family system as a factor of Domestic Violence

Age	Yes	No
18-35 years	20	**11**
36-50 years	16	8
51-75 years	11	
Total	47	28
Percentage	62.6	37.4

From the data collected as shown in the above table above 62.6% of the respondents representing the age groups between 18 to 75 years agree that the shift from Joint family to Nuclear family system is one of the causes of domestic violence. The table also reveals that an absolute majority i.e. 76% of the respondents who agree to the above idea belong to the younger and middle age group categories. Therefore, this substantiates the actuality that the shift from joint to nuclear family system is a recent phenomenon in the Khasi society. This can be seen especially in the urban areas where most people have adopted a nuclear family system where the husband, wife and children are part of it. The fact, that most of the respondents are urban-based as shown in table no. A. gives impetus to the above argument. This is unlike the traditional Joint family where the wife's parents, maternal uncles, sisters and brothers lived together. In the traditional family system it is the maternal uncle who makes most of the decisions pertaining to the family matters. In present time this role is occupied by the father (see foot note no. 28). Therefore, the power of decision making is vested in his hands. This may lead to the mechanism of control and domination leading to domestic violence. Commenting on this aspect, Rica Lamar opines that the women have a support system and early intervention where problems can be resolved faster in the joint family. She continues to say that in a nuclear family most of the time only two people are involved and most problems or conflicts cannot be resolved quickly resulting in domestic violence.,[20] Nevertheless, this factor cannot be generalized as there are many families in the rural set up who still follow the joint family system, yet they are not free from domestic violence. However, the shift from joint to nuclear family system is one of the factors giving rise to domestic violence in the present Khasi society.

3.6.4. Patriarchy and Power as Controlling Mechanisms Perpetrating Domestic Violence

Patriarchy and power are interlinked because of the close association they have with one another. They are often used as controlling mechanisms by the powerful against the powerless. It is men, who often use patriarchy and power as tools to dominate, subjugate and manipulate women in the society and family. As per the study conducted the Khasi matrilineal society practices patriarchy and most men use power to violate the rights and dignity of women. Patriarchy and Power are therefore, looked at as main ideological factors that perpetuate violence against women in the domestic set up.

3.6.4.1. Patriarchy in Matriliny

Patriarchy as an ideological and psychological factor is one of the crucial reasons for perpetrating domestic violence against women mainly in patriarchal societies. Nevertheless, this factor also operates within the Khasi matrilineal system to oppress, subjugate and marginalize women in many ways. The following table shows that patriarchy is the key factor for domestic violence against women in the Khasi matrilineal society.

Table No. F. V. Patriarchy as a factor causing Domestic Violence

Gender	Yes	No
Male	28	9
Female	26	12
Total	54	21
Percentage	72.0	28.0

20 Interview with Rica Lamar.

Patriarchy as discussed in the previous chapter is one of the contributing factors towards domestic violence. The table above exposes that an absolute majority i.e. 72% of the respondents agree that the Khasi matrilineal society is practicing patriarchal values in many ways. This fact substantiate the argument that power is used as a controlling mechanism by men whether in the family or society. It is interesting to note that the above table shows that most of the male respondents agree that the Khasi society practices patriarchy. This goes on to show that patriarchy is deeply rooted in the Khasi mindset projecting itself in cultural, political and religious dimensions. Commenting on this, Roshan Warjri opines everything is not well in the matrilineal society where women were held with high esteem. She further argues that going deep into the matter would reveal other distressing factors that need to be immediately redressed. About 35% of the married women had to face domestic violence in one form or the other. She further asserts that though it is a matrilineal society, it is patriarchal in many ways.[21] Patriarchy is the main agendum by which men perpetuates domestic violence against women in the Khasi society. Power and domination plays an important role in this regard.[22] The Khasi society except for lineage is patriarchal in many regards, for instance decision making is a male profession till today. Women are still debarred from participating in political and religious circles. The church and society is turning a deaf ear to their grievances. Therefore, it can be said that the Khasi society practice patriarchy and therefore perpetuates domestic violence against women. The table below substantiates the above argument that power in terms of patriarchy is used to dominate and perpetuate domestic violence against women in the Khasi matrilineal society.

3.6.4.2. Power as a tool of Domination

Power here means domination and control or power is used as a tool for domination and control by the powerful against the powerless.

---

[21] "Meghalaya's matrilineal society faces domestic violence," *The Shillong Times* (Shillong), 20 August 2004, 1.

[22] Interview with Annie Sohtun, Social Worker, North East Network, Shillong, 26 May, 2009.

Culture and religion sanction men as more powerful than women. Therefore they exercised this power to dominate women in the society and family. Power also has a connection with patriarchy where through the ideology of patriarchy power is manifested. Power is therefore associated with domestic violence as men used it as a controlling mechanism to control and silent women through the use of violence. The table below shows that power is used as a controlling mechanism in the society or family to perpetuate domestic violence against women in the Khasi matrilineal society.

Table No. F. VI. Power as a controlling mechanism perpetuating Domestic Violence

Gender	Yes	No
Male	22	15
Female	32	6
Total	54	21
Percentage	72.0	28.0

An overwhelming majority i.e. 72% of the respondents comprising of both male and female agree that Power is associated with domestic violence. The above table also shows that majority of the respondents who agree that power is associated with domestic violence are female. This verifies that most women in the Khasi society are being dominated and controlled by men in their families. As stated, power is used as an authority to control and dictate the other, which may be executed by the dominant partner on the subordinate. In most cases it is the men who use power as a controlling mechanism over women. The controlling of women is exhibited through power explicitly shown in terms of violence. This is another contributing factor towards domestic violence in the Khasi matrilineal society.

3.7. Divorce and Suicide: The Extreme Steps Victims of Domestic Violence resort to

Divorce and suicide are considered as the extreme steps that the victims of domestic violence resort to. The table below precisely shows this fact.

Table No. G. I. The Extreme Steps Victims of Domestic Violence resort to

Marital status	Divorce	Suicide	Both Divorce & Suicide
Married	22	3	9
Unmarried	19	6	8
Widow	2	0	0
Total	43	9	17
Percentage	62.4	13.0	24.6

The above table emphasizes on the issue whether victims of domestic violence resort to divorce, suicide or both of these. Majority of the respondents i.e. 62.4% of them opine that victims of domestic violence resort to divorce. However, only 13% think that they resort to suicide and 24.6% agree that they may end in both divorce and suicide. Nevertheless, the consensus as per the observation above is that divorce is the most likely possibility the victims of domestic violence resort to. Patricia Mukhim is of the view that divorce is most likely to happen but in extreme cases of depression it may also lead to suicide or attempt to suicide. She further argues that since the Khasi do not have a strong binding law of marriage in many cases, therefore, separation is more common rather than divorce which requires legal intervention.[23] On the other hand Rica Lamar opines

[23] Interview with Patricia Mukhim. In the present Khasi society people do not have a strong binding law of marriage. Therefore, most men are likely to abandon their partner after a certain period of time leaving behind the children to be looked after by the wife alone or her parents and relatives. In most cases the woman has to look after her children alone without seeking the help of her parents as she is considered as a trespasser or someone who have done something very sinful owing

divorce or separation may occur as a last resort after years of abuse and violence, women take up this extreme step.[24] In any case we can infer that most women resort to divorce or separation from their husband. However, the vital question which arises here is who is the most vulnerable victim of this tragedy? The table below answers this question.

3.7.1. Children as Victims of Domestic Violence

Divorce or suicide has a repercussion on the children and their future. They become the most vulnerable victims of domestic violence. The table below discloses this actuality.

Table No. G. II. Children as Victims of Domestic Violence

Marital status	Wife	Husband	Children	Wife and Children
Married	2	1	28	5
Unmarried	1	0	31	5
Widow	1	0	0	1
Total	4	1	59	**11**
Percentage	5.3	1.3	78.7	14.7

The table above discloses that an overwhelming majority i.e. 78.7% of the respondents think that children are the worst affected victims of domestic violence. If divorce or separation occurs children suffer the consequences. If the male member leaves or abandons the family which is very obvious in the Khasi society as discussed earlier because of no legal binding bond of marriage, it leaves to the female to look after her family and children. Children's future is really affected and sometime if a woman is unemployed, it may also leads to other problems like prostitution[25] where a woman in order

to the reason that parents may not be pleased with the marriage. This may lead to further complications as seen in the present Khasi society where women supported families or single parenting is very common.

[24] Interview with Rica Lamar.

[25] Interview with Patricia Mukhim.

to support her children has to take up this step. Therefore, what we see is, domestic violence in itself leads to many complications like divorce or separation and if that happen it affects the children's life and also affecting the woman's dignity and future.

3.8. Reporting Cases of Domestic Violence

How far are all the cases of domestic violence being positively reported to the police or the local durbar or council? The table below shows the idea of how cases of domestic violence are reported in their respective localities/villages.

Table No. H. I. Reporting Cases of Domestic Violence

Gender	Cases are reported to the local durbar		Cases are reported to the police		Through the role of media		Through the role of various NGOs	
	Yes	No	Yes	No	Yes	No	Yes	No
Male	12	25	7	30	34	3	16	21
Female	6	32	13	25	28	10	23	15
Total	18	57	20	55	62	13	39	36
Percentage	24.0	76.0	26.7	73.3	82.7	17.3	52.0	48.0

From the above table it is vividly clear that two thirds i.e. 82.7% of the respondents come to know about domestic violence through the role of media, which includes print and visual media. This idea substantiates the data showed in the table no. C.II. where most of the respondents learnt about domestic violence from the media. This is obvious since most of the respondents are educated as per table no. B.II. As we can see from the above table, local durbar or council or the police have the marginal role to play in this regard. The reasons for that will be discussed below. Furthermore, more than half i.e. 52% of the respondents agree that they come to know about domestic violence through the role of various NGO's working on domestic violence and related issues.

3.8.1. Reporting Cases of Domestic Violence to the Police

Most of the time cases of domestic violence are not reported to the police owing to the fear or stigma associated with it. The following table indicates this dimension.

Table No. H. II. Reporting cases of domestic violence to the Police

Qualification	Yes	No
Under Matric	0	3
Secondary/Higher Secondary	1	9
Graduate	3	33
Post Graduate	2	23
Above Post Graduate	0	1
Total	6	69
Percentage	8.0	92.0

The above table indicates that an absolute majority i.e. 92% of the respondents on the basis of educational qualifications opine that many cases of domestic violence are not reported to the police. This reveals the fact that most of the cases go unreported. The year wise crime against women reported during 2007-2017 on protection of women against domestic violence from Domestic Violence Act, 2005 is zero.[26] The question arise why is this so? Why cases of domestic violence are not reported? The reasons are given below as per the findings of the study conducted.

3.8.1.1. Reasons for not reporting cases of Domestic Violence to the Police

The table below gives the reasons as to why most of the cases of domestic violence are not reported to the police.

[26] http://www.megpolice.gov.in>crime_statistics.html, accessed 6 March, 2019.

Table No. H. III. Reasons for not reporting cases of Domestic Violence to the Police.

Qualification	Taken as personal matter		Brings Dishonor to the family	
	Yes	No	Yes	No
Under Matric	3	0	2	1
Secondary/Higher Secondary	6	4	6	4
Graduate	21	15	24	12
Post Graduate	19	6	16	9
Above Post Graduate	0	1	0	1
Total	49	26	48	27
Percentage	65.3	34.7	64.0	36.0

The above table shows two important reasons why cases of domestic violence are not reported to the police. About 65.3% of the respondents believe that domestic violence is a personal matter and another 64% of them opine that it brings dishonor to the family. Therefore most cases go unreported. This goes on to show that in the Khasi society domestic violence is still a hidden issue. The above table also reveals the fact that most people are still having a stigma of reporting cases of domestic violence to the police as they think it is a personal or family matter which should be dealt within the family. Theilin Phanbuh states that shame and fear are preventing the Khasi women from reporting domestic violence either to the police or law. She further opines that this has to do more with the culture of silence most women embrace in order to protect the dignity of the family by suffering themselves.[27]

3.8.2. Local Durbar (Council) and Domestic Violence

The table below indicates as to whether the local durbar (council) plays any role when cases of domestic violence are reported in the respective localities /villages.

[27] Interview with Theilin Phanbuh, Social Worker, Shillong, 2 June, 2009. (Here after cited as Interview with Theilin Phanbuh).

Table No. H. IV. Local Durbar (Council) and Domestic Violence

Gender	Yes	No
Male	15	22
Female	15	23
Total	30	45
Percentage	40.0	60.0

From the above table it can be argued that the local durbar do not play an active role when cases of domestic violence are reported. More than half i.e. 60% agree that their local durbar or council do not play an active role when cases of domestic violence are reported. D.S Mawlong asserts that the reason why the local durbar (Council) does not interfere in these cases is because people are not free to report them positively due to the fear of more violence in the future.[28] Therefore, most of these cases are solved within the context of the family or the victims are silenced owing to fear and stigma associated with the outcome of violence.

In the following table we will see why the local durbar (council) does not take proper steps in counter acting cases of domestic violence in their respective localities.

3.8.2.1. Reasons why Local Durbar (Council) do not take active part in cases of domestic violence

The following table indicates the reasons as to why the local durbar (council) does not take active part when cases of domestic violence are reported in their respective localities or villages.

[28] Interview with D.S. Mawlong.

Table No. H. V. Reasons why Local Durbar (Council) does not take active part in cases of Domestic Violence

Gender	Taken as personal matter		No sufficient law enacted	
	Yes	No	Yes	No
Male	23	14	32	5
Female	22	16	33	5
Total	45	30	65	10
Percentage	60.0	40.0	86.7	13.3

The above table reveals the obvious reasons why local durbar (council) does not take active part when cases of domestic violence are reported. Firstly, domestic violence is taken as a personal or family matter which should not be interfered and secondly, no laws are enacted in the respective locality to deal with domestic violence. More than half i.e. 60% of the respondents agree that local durbar do not interfere in cases of domestic violence as they are taken to be personal or family matters. Two thirds i.e. 86.7% of the respondents believe that the local durbar (council) do not have laws enacted with regard to domestic violence. This goes on to show that the Khasi society is not open to this issue till today and it remains a matter in the closed door.

3.9. Law and Domestic Violence

There are many legal measures associated with domestic violence (as discussed in Chapter Two, sub section 2.5.). The most important and recent one is the Protection of Women from Domestic Violence Act, 2005. The following table discloses the fact as to whether this Act is enough to tackle the problem of domestic violence in each locality or village.

Table No. I. Law and Domestic Violence

Age	Yes	No
18-35 years	9	22
36-50 years	6	**18**
51-74 years	8	12
Total	23	52
Percentage	30.7	69.3

Considering the figures in the above table, it is clear that the Protection of Women from Domestic Violence (PWDV) Act, 2005 is not sufficient to protect women from domestic violence. About 69.3% of the respondents agree to this fact. Though, most of the respondents belong to the educated class as seen in the table no. B.II. but the above figures show that they are unaware of the above Act. Furthermore, 76.9% of the respondents who are not aware of this Act belong to the age group between 18-50 years. This goes on to show that the younger and the middle age group categories are ignorant of the Act. Therefore, the apparent reason why many respondents think that the Act on domestic violence is not enough to deal with the issue shows that the people are still uninformed about the above Act. Thus, they do not take advantage of this Act. For that reason, awareness programs should be conducted especially at the grass root level, where the Government or the NGO's concerned should take up the matter seriously.[29] Furthermore, Khasi women do not want to take up any legal help because of the stigma and fear associated with it. They are not free to report or take the assistance of the law as they think it will bring disgrace to their family.[30] Moreover, some of the loopholes of this Act are that medical examinations are most of the time delayed, there is a judicial delay and there is no family court for domestic violence formed till today in Meghalaya.[31] It may also be noted that till October 2008, there are only four cases under PWDV

[29] Interview with Patricia Mukhim.

[30] Interview with Theilin Phanbuh.

[31] Interview with Rica Lamar.

Act being registered in Ri-Bhoi and East Khasi Hills Districts.[32] This reveals that people are still uninformed and have not utilized this Act properly considering the amount and rateof domestic violence in the present Khasi society.

3.10. Men as Victims Domestic Violence

We have seen that most of the victims of domestic violence in the Khasi matrilineal society are women (section 3.5.1., table no. E.I.). Domestic against women often leads to divorce and suicide (section 3.7.1. table no. G.I.) and children are also victimized in the process (sub section 3.7.1.1., table no. G.IL). The following table indicates as to whether men are also victims of domestic violence in the Khasi matrilineal society.

Table No. J. Men as Victims Domestic Violence

Gender	Yes	No
Male	20	17
Female	30	8
Total	50	25
Percentage	66.7	33.3

Among many research works carried on in many western societies, it may be surprising to know the presence of male as victims of domestic violence. Conway argued that male victims are not always visible as female victims as they have more economic power and apart from that the society is less accepting to recognize them as victims.[33] In the Khasi matrilineal society it is visible from the above table that men too are victims of domestic violence. More than half i.e. 66.7% of the respondents agree that men are victims of domestic violence in some form or the other. It may also be noted, that, the above table indicates that most number of respondents who agree that men are victims of domestic violence are women.

[32] "Domestic violence not alarming," *The Shillong Times* (Shillong), 28 November, 2008, 3.

[33] Conway, *Domestic Violence and the Church...*, 8.

This goes on to show that in the Khasi society both the sexes face domestic violence. However, many opine that violence against men in the domestic set up is more emotional or verbal in nature. Patricia Mukhim commenting on this says that men especially who happen to marry the youngest daughter *(Khatduh)* often face verbal violence from his in-laws, especially when he is either unemployed or having a low income. In fact he is discriminated mentally and emotionally.'[34] This often leads to frustration in men which at times result in alcoholism. On the other hand Sweetie Diengdoh argues that even if domestic violence against men takes place in one form or the other yet no cases are known to have been reported till date.[35] Nevertheless, the fact is that men are facing domestic violence in the Khasi society. Perhaps the important thing to be noted is that even though domestic violence against men is present in the Khasi matrilineal society, nonetheless, it is not as widespread as that of women. On the other hand, 33.3% of the respondents opine that men do not face domestic violence. It is interesting to note that the above table discloses that most of the respondents who do not agree that men are victimized in their families are men themselves. This shows that men themselves are not ready either to accept themselves as victims of domestic violence or they are hiding the issue because of the fear of losing status and reputation in the society.

3.11. Countering Domestic Violence

Domestic violence has marred the Khasi matrilineal society in different degrees and forms as we have seen from the above data collected. The question arise how can it be countered? Are there ways and means to do so? No doubt concerned governmental and non-governmental organizations and the Church have their respective roles in this regard. In the following paragraphs we will emphasize on this aspect to see as to whether domestic violence has been countered positively or not, giving the fact of its intensity in the present Khasi matrilineal society.

---

[34] Interview with Patricia Mukhim.

[35] Interview with Sweetie Diengdoh, Retired Government Servant, Shillong, 29 May, 2009.

3.11.1. The Role of Media

Media, whether print or visual play an important role in combating domestic violence. The following table explicates the role of media in countering domestic violence in the Khasi society.

Table No. K. I. The Role of Media in Countering Domestic Violence

Qualification	Yes	No
Under Matric	3	0
Secondary/ Higher Secondary	9	1
Graduate	33	3
Post Graduate	23	2
Above Post Graduate	1	0
Total	69	6
Percentage	92.0	8.0

From the above table it be inferred that an absolute majority i.e. 92% of the respondents agree that the local print media and visual media play a positive and significant role in reporting cases of domestic violence. This verifies the data in the table no. C.IL, where most people become aware of domestic violence through Newspaper and table no. H.L, which reveals the most cases of domestic violence are reported through print and visual media. The local print media includes the various local daily newspapers like *The Shillong Times, Meghalaya Guardian, U Mawphor* and *U Nongsain Hima* to name few. The local visual media includes the local news channels like the Doordarshan Kendra Shillong, the Peitngor Cable News (PCN) and others. B.R. Kharlukhi agrees that print and local media are looked upon as eyes and ears, bringing to light the intensity of domestic violence taking place everywhere, therefore, building a positive public awareness on the issue.[36] Still further, Rica Lamar asserts that though she agrees to the fact that local and print media play a positive role in reporting cases of domestic violence, yet the media has to give proper and accurate information not to defame the victims at all.[37] Thus,

[36] Interview with B.R. Kharlukhi, Church Elder, Shillong, 16 September, 2012.

[37] Interview with Rica Lamar.

media both local print and visual media though playing a positive and proactive role in reporting domestic violence but the process of reporting should be correct and never try to denigrate the image and dignity of the victims.

3.11.2. The Role of Government

The government has a pivotal responsibility to thwart against domestic violence. The following table indicates as to whether the government has taken appropriate steps in combating against domestic violence in the Khasi society.

Table No. K. II. The Role of Government in combating Domestic Violence

Qualification	Yes	No
Under Matric	3	0
Secondary/Higher Secondary	3	7
Graduate	17	19
Post Graduate	8	17
Above Post Graduate	0	1
Total	31	44
Percentage	41.3	58.7

Table above indicates that more than half of the respondents, i.e., 58.7% are of the view that the government is not doing enough to combat domestic violence. However, another 41.3% think that the Government has taken appropriate steps to counteract domestic violence. I.D. Lyngwa says that the government has taken sufficient steps to counter domestic violence. She further mention that steps like awareness programs, counseling and working with other non-governmental organizations on the issue are being done in recent past.'[38] Nevertheless it can be argued that many of the respondents comprising of the educated class are not aware of the steps taken

[38] Interview with I.D Lyngwa, The District Social Welfare Officer, Shillong, 2 May, 2009.

by the government because of the lack of sensitization or awareness on the issue. Theilin Phanbuh opines that nothing much can be done by the government as most cases are not reported to the concerned officers looking on the matter.[39] Therefore, the process of conscientization on the issue to the masses not just among the educated section but at the grass root level is the first priority which is then followed by other legal aids and measures are indeed the need of the hour.

3.11.3. The Role of Non-Governmental Organizations

The table below clarifies whether Non Governmental Organizations (NGO's) play any role in dealing with the problem of domestic violence.

Table No. K. III. The Role of Non-Governmental Organizations infighting against Domestic Violence

Qualification	Yes	No
Under Matric	1	2
Secondary/ Higher Secondary	8	2
Graduate	25	11
Post Graduate	20	5
Above Post Graduate	1	0
Total	55	20
Percentage	73.3	26.7

The above table reveals that 73.3 percent of the respondents agree that the NGOs are playing a role in countering domestic violence in the Khasi society. Nevertheless, the table H.I., shows almost half of the respondents i.e. 48% feel that NGOs do not play a prominent role in reporting cases of domestic violence. This goes on to show even though majority of the respondents agree that NGOs play a role in countering domestic violence, but the process of awareness and conscientization is not being substantially dealt with.

[39] Interview with Theilin Phanbuh.

North East Network (NEN), Civil Society Women Organization (CSWO) and *Ka Synjuk Ki Seng Kynthei* (a culmination of many organizations working on women' issues) are some important NGOs apart from others, working on women' issues especially on Violence against Women including domestic violence. Rica Lamar opines that the reason why NGOs are more active in this regard is due to the fact that most victims of domestic violence find it easier to approach them than any other means. Cases are then referred to the Social Welfare Office and to the State women Commission for further help rendered to the victims.[40] Apart from these NGOs, there are de-addiction and counseling centers like Sanker Rehabilitation center, Bosco Reach Out, Kripa, New Hope Center and others which are actively working in monitoring the problem of alcoholism and drug addiction, which is more or less related to domestic violence. However, as stated domestic violence remains a silent issue in many families and NGOs has an important responsibility to see that the issue is adequately tackled.

3.11.4. The Role of the Church

The church has a prominent task to counter the malady of domestic violence. The answer whether the church plays a role in fighting against domestic violence in the Khasi matrilineal society is given below:

Table No. K. IV. The Role of the Church in responding to Domestic Violence

Age	Yes	No
18-35 years	9	22
36-50 years	8	16
51-75 years	7	13
Total	24	51
Percentage	32.0	68.0

Majority of the respondents about 68 % who belong to the age group between 18 to 75 years of age do not agree that the Church

[40] Interview with Rica Lamar.

is taking an active role in countering domestic violence. Most of the respondents belong to the younger and middle age group categories. This substantiates the fact presented in table no. C.IL, where domestic violence is not a matter of concern for the church or it is not the source from where people learnt about domestic violence. This is visible that the church is keeping aloof from this issue or it remains to be a silent spectator. The reason is that the Church is emphasizing too much on spiritual life than the real life situation which people encounter.[41] On the other hand, 38.7% of the respondents agree that the church is taking steps to deal with domestic violence in the Khasi society. At most what the Church do is to provide counseling and prayer to the affected families, that also in special cases when either informed or requested. The reasons why the church is not playing an active role in countering domestic violence are given below:

3.11.4.1. Reasons why the Church do not play a role in countering Domestic Violence

The following table indicates the reasons as to why the church does not play an active role in combating domestic violence.

Table No. K. V. Reasons why the Church does not play a role in opposing Domestic Violence

Age	Domestic violence is new to the Church		The Church should not interfere as it is a personal matter		No cases of domestic violence known to the Church	
	Yes	No	Yes	No	Yes	No
18-27 years	10	14	14	10	1	23
28-36 years	9	16	17	8	1	24
37-75 years	10	16	14	12	2	24
Total	29	46	45	30	4	71
Percentage	38.7	61.3	60.0	40.0	5.3	94.7

41 Interview with B.R. Kharlukhi.

If we carefully study the above table indicates that more than half i.e. 60% of the respondents opine that the obvious reason why the church is not playing an active role in countering domestic violence is because it is believed that, it should not interfere with it as it is taken as a personal or family matter. It is also to be noted that majority of the respondents, who agree to this belong to the age group between 18-50 years. This goes on to show that the younger and the middle age generations see the church as concentrating mostly on spiritual and institutional matters, sidelining itself from the issues of the day.

Therefore, it seems the mentality of the Khasi society or church connotes the same ideology of denying the issue as it is a personal matter. This indeed calls for a radical shift if we are to counteract domestic violence positively in the Khasi society in general and Church in particular. Steps should be taken to conscientize and help in bringing about a solution to this problem. If we observe the table carefully about 94.7% of the respondents agree that cases of domestic violence are known to the church, and on the same line 61.3% of them opine that it is not a new issue. Nonetheless, it did not play any active and positive role in countering this problem. This shows that the church is playing the role of a silent spectator.

From the above, we can argue that some measures are taken by the government in countering domestic violence through certain procedures. The various NGOs are doing their bit to deal with the issue concretely. The role of the church is still very doubtful in this regard. Nevertheless, to counteract this problem concretely and positively these organizations along with the civil society must take steps to deal and to attempt in finding possible solutions in order to stop this menace which is fast growing in many Khasi families today.

Conclusion

From the above study and analysis of the data collected, we can pose the following concluding remarks. Firstly, domestic violence is an issue of concern in the Khasi matrilineal society, affecting most families today. Secondly, women are the main targets of violence which nullify the common belief that in matrilineal society women enjoy a much better status or are more respected than their counterparts in patriarchal societies. In fact, domestic violence is a reality in any society today and women are the victims. The types or forms of domestic violence women suffer most include physical, verbal, sexual and emotional. The intensity and form of violence may differ from one case to another. On the other side, it is also seen that men too can be victims of domestic violence in the Khasi matrilineal society, nevertheless, the intensity and form of violence is not so severe like that of women. Men mostly suffer verbal and emotional or psychological violence. Furthermore, most cases are either not reported or denied owing to the stigma of loosing their male status. Thirdly, we have also seen that there are many factors that contribute to the rise of cases of domestic violence in the Khasi society; nonetheless, significant ones are situational and psychological factors like alcoholism, unemployment/poverty and extra-marital affairs. Other factors are pornography, patriarchy and power differentials and shift from joint to nuclear family system. Fourthly, we could also argue that in most cases victims of domestic violence resort to divorce or separation which adversely affect the children and also the whole economy of the family which leads to further problem like single parenting and prostitution. Fifthly, we also see that most cases are not reported to the police or law as there is still a stigma that domestic violence is taken as a family or personal matter. Finally, the study reveals that government is not doing enough to find out ways and means to counteract this issue, and cases of violence against women especially at family level in on the rise. There is a need for the process of conscientization of the existing laws and privileges to the general masses and women in particular right from the grass root level. The church in the Khasi society did not play much role on this issue; therefore, it is an urgent need for it to express itself towards this concern if it is to build a community of equality, peace and justice. In fact the whole civil society needs to find out ways and means to counter this issue concretely and positively.

The whole discussion on domestic violence in the Khasi matrilineal society needs to be addressed deeply. As per the study conducted and the data analyzed there are many important reasons that contribute to the rise of domestic violence. An in-depth analysis of the data collected reveals that there is a specific ideology which acts as *a prima facie* reason for the cause of domestic violence in the Khasi matrilineal society. Patriarchy is actually the root cause which has been ideologically and wisely passed on for ages now in the Khasi society. It functions as the base from where men actually exercise their power to dominate and control women through the use of violence in the family. It is through this ideology that other factors sprang out to perpetuate violence against women in the domestic and societal set up. The whole issue revolves around the question, who controls what and whom? As stated, except for few privileges given to the women in terms of lineage and descent there are no specific areas where women are given place to exercise their rights and privileges. This in fact proves that the assumption of the Khasi society as a society that gives more space and status to women is actually wrong. They remain silent in many issues including the process of decision making which is still a male profession whether in the society or the church till today. A concrete and viable response should therefore address this aspect in a more appropriate and befitting manner. Perhaps one of the main reasons to counteract this is to create a just relationship in the society at large and family in particular. Justice, equality and liberation through right relationship in the society and family is the dictum. This has to be the focal point if we are to talk of an inclusive society free of discrimination and violence against each other as fellow human beings.

Chapter 4

KAMAI IA KA HOK (EARN RIGHTEOUSNESS): TOWARDS AN INDIGENOUS THEOLOGICAL-ETHICAL RESPONSE TO DOMESTIC VIOLENCE IN THE KHASI MATRILINEAL SOCIETY

Introduction

In the previous chapter, we have noted that domestic violence has affected the Khasi society. This certainly needs a concrete and feasible response. The researcher is proposing a Khasi indigenous theological-ethical response. For this, the Khasi concept *Kamai ia ka Hok* (earn righteousness} is used as a theological-ethical frame to evolve certain criteria which are employed to respond to the above problem. *Kamai ia ka Hok is* a Khasi indigenous religious-ethical norm which shaped the social, political, economic and religious life of the Khasi in the past. However, this is neglected if not forgotten in the present Khasi society. It is thus, apt to re-capture and re-interpret its ethical values, pertaining to the Khasi society as a whole and particularly to the issue of domestic violence. The researcher also poses a challenge to the Khasi society and church in particular to re-visit this important concept in constructing a viable Khasi indigenous theological-ethical thinking. This will also operate as a process of conscientization of the importance of this concept for the well being and functioning of the Khasi society.

4.1. Defining and Conceptualizing the term *Kamai ia ka Hok* (earn righteousness)

Literally *Kamai ia ka Hok* means 'to earn righteousness'. *Kamai* means 'to earn' and *Hok* stands for righteousness. However, the Khasi understanding does not mean righteousness alone but it also connotes idea like justice and rightness. This term may also to be translated as 'to strive for righteousness'. The Khasi believe that their life in this world is to strive for righteousness and to do justice. Righteousness sprang out of the idea of right and just relationship with God and fellow human beings. To do this he/she has to respect and act fairly in his/her relationship to God and human beings through his/her deeds. According to R. Tokin Rymbai, God sent human beings into this world for the purpose of earning or striving for righteousness through their actions towards other fellow beings and this must be guided by Ka *Hok* i.e. righteousness.[1] Kelian Synrem further elaborates that the model of earning righteousness means that human beings are born with *Ka Hok* (righteousness) and *Ka Hukum Blei* (God's Command), nevertheless, these intrinsic values can be realized by putting them into practice. For her therefore, *Ka Hok* here stands for an upright life in relation to God and fellow human beings.[2] Thus, this term is very crucial in the life of the Khasi. It implies a concept that characterizes justice, right and responsible relationship or action, equality, liberation and acts as a yard stick for the cultural, social, economic and religious ethos of the Khasi.

4.2. The Khasi Understanding of *Ka Hok* (righteousness)

The word *Hok is* translated as righteousness. According to J.K. Tariang, *Ka Hok* or righteousness in the life of the Khasi would mean

---

[1] R. Tokin Rymbai, *Ban Pynieng La Ka Rasong bad Kiwei Kiwei de ki Ese* (Shillong: Witibon Hynniewta Rymbai, 1979), 46.

[2] Kelian Synrem, "Religion of the Khasis," *Seng Khasi Souvenir: 100 Years Celebration, 1899-1999* (Shillong: Seng Khasi, 1999), 109-112, here 109.

the truth, something reasonable, something good, the right way and a quality that does not support partiality or any kind of oppression.[3] According to the Khasi folklore, God keeps human beings in this world and made a covenant with them. This covenant reads *"ieng rangbah u briew ha tbian ap jutang u Blei haneng"* (human being should strive for justice on earth while God in heaven expect for the accomplishment of this covenant). Therefore, as long as human beings live on this earth they should seek righteousness in terms of justice in all spheres of life. R.T. Rymbai comments that the Khasi way of life was based in this aspect of *Hok* for personal, social, political and economic life. *Ka Hok* is the goal that every individual sought in their everyday life. To ignore this, is to ignore the very purpose that God has for every human being.'[4]

The notion of *Hok* (righteousness) in the Khasi understanding is the offshoot of one of the Khasi legends. According to this legend there was a 'heavenly ladder' at a peak called *U Sohpetbneng* (the navel of heaven).[5] The ladder is believed to connect heaven and earth. Therefore, there was free movement between heaven and earth. It was also believed that the Khasi comprised of sixteen families, who used to descend between heaven and earth through this ladder. They came down in the morning to cultivate in the land and go back in the evening. But a time came where this connection was cut off by the seven families. It was from that moment that human beings started to face diseases, various problems and even face the bitterness of death.[6] It was in this context that the notion of Ka *Hok* plays a very key role. In order to get back to that which was lost, human being is called to strive for righteousness. In order to do this, human has to build right and just relationship with fellow human beings and God. Therefore, the other aspect of *Kamai ia ka Hok* (earning righteousness) is to establish

[3] J.K. Tariang, "Kamai ia ka Hok," *Sneng Khasi* 73/10 (November 1997), 15-21.

[4] R.T. Rymbai, "U HynniewTrep bad la ka Niam," *Seng Khasi Souvenir* (Shillong: Seng Khasi, 1986), 12.

[5] B.C. Lyngdoh, "The Concept of God in the Khasi Tradition and its Implications for Christianity" (Unpublished B.D. Thesis, Senate of Serampore College, 1976), 16-17.

[6] H.W. Sten, *Ka History ka Ktien Khasi* (Shillong: Self, 1980), 39.

this broken relationship, through justice, mutual respect, right and responsible relationship with fellow humans which culminates in establishing right relationship with God.

Speaking on this concept Sib Charan Roy opines that *Hok* refers to all deeds that are good, righteous, just and which brings welfare to every human beings.[7] Therefore, good and righteous deeds here refer to the 'good' in terms of relationship which puts other human being as the centre for all kinds of action. *Ka Hok is* a benchmark for the Khasi social, economic and political ethos. In this concept, human become the focal point for establishing justice and peace in this world which thus, becomes a maxim for right relationship with God.

4.3. *Kamai ia ka Hok* (earn righteousness): Its Relationship to other Religious Ethical Norms

The concept of *Kamai ia Hok* (earn righteousness) has a very deep and crucial relationship with the other Religious-Ethical Norms, which therefore, has a tremendous impact on the social, cultural, economic, political and religious life of the Khasi (some of these Religious-Ethical norms or teachings have been discussed briefly in Chapter One, sub section 1.6.1.). Nevertheless, this section stresses on their relationship with one another and their importance in the Khasi society. The point to be noted here is that these concepts or norms are slowly diminishing from the psyche of the present Khasi society, accordingly, the need to revive and re-interpret their theological-ethical validity for the Khasi society.

4.3.1. *Tip Briew Tip Blei* (Know Human Know God)

Tip is translated as `to know'; *Briew* stands for human beings and *Blei* mean God. Therefore *Tip Briew Tip Blei* literally means 'to know human, to know God' or in other words, it may also be translated as 'to know our fellow human beings is to know God' or still further 'to know the other is to know God' or 'human consciousness is God consciousness.' Rymbai comments that the importance of

[7] Sib Charan Roy, *Ka Niam Ki Khasi, Ka Niam Tip Briew Tip Blei,* 1919 Reprint (Shillong: Ri Khasi Press, 2003), viii.

this concept is that human can only know God when he/she know or respect his/her fellow human beings. Knowing a fellow human being would mean performance of one's responsibility towards them through good, kind and helpful actions to one and all and not to cause harm or do any his/her identity and status in the society.'[8] So, a Khasi would always make sure that he/she respects his/her maternal and paternal relations, which then reflect the relationship in the society and family in particular. A person who do not know the norm or teaching of *Tip Kur Tip Kha* would never know God or his/her fellow human beings and would therefore never earn righteousness in his/her life. Thus, it is implicit that this norm governs the relationship in the family in particular and society in general. This is actually the command of God to the Khasi to live a life of righteousness in terms of his/her dealings with other fellow humans starting from his/her family and relation first and then to the society and the whole cosmos.

4.3.3. *Tip Akor Tip Burom (Know* the Etiquettes of Life)

The Khasi are very conscious about the system of etiquettes. In fact, children are being instructed on social manners and behaviors right from their early days by their parents. Mawrie comments that the Khasi words *burom* and *akor* do not mean only good manners but imply decency in conduct and behavior. For this reason these terms carry a certain degree of moral implications in them."[9] This norm or teaching is related to the idea of right action and relationship with the other person. Therefore, like the other norms or teachings also impacted the Khasi understanding of relationship in terms of justice, peace and right action in all aspects of life. The idea is to respect the right and dignity of the other person and never to practice injustice of any kind. Thus, to do this a Khasi has to know the etiquettes of life in respecting and honoring the other fellow human beings. To injustice for one's own whims and fancies.[10] So, knowing God in the Khasi understanding is to know fellow human beings. There

---

[8] Barnes L. Mawrie, *Introduction to Khasi Ethics...*, 24-25.

[9] *Ibid.*, 25-26.

[10] R.T. Rymbai, "Some Aspects of the Religion of the Khasi Pnars..." 112.

is a vertical and horizontal relationship between human-God and human-human respectively. Thus, the Khasi stress on maintaining this relationship which is right, just and honest in every aspects of their life. Therefore, *Tip Briew Tip Blei is* a religious-ethical teaching or norm of the Khasi which govern their social, cultural, economic, political and religious dimensions of life. It is very close to the concept of *Kamai ia ka Hok,* since it emphasizes on maintaining just, fair and right relationship among fellow human beings and between human and God. Hence, it actually acts as a standard for determining the relationship which God wanted each human to observe in order for the *Hok* (righteousness) to be established in the society and all spheres of life.

4.3.2. *Tip Kur Tip Kha* (Know one's own Maternal and Paternal Relations)

Tip Kur Tip Kha literally means 'to know one's own maternal and paternal relations. Since the Khasi society is a matrilineal society as discussed earlier, descend is traced from the mother. The ancestral mother is known as *Ka Iawbei* and all her descendants form *Ka Kur* (clan). It is considered to be a sin *(ka sang)* to marry within the same clan. Thus, it is imperative for the Khasi to know the members of their own clan. There is a healthy relationship of a person with *Ki Kur* (members of the same clan) and *Ki Kha* (members of the father's clan). This norm forms the basic ethical outlook for the Khasi. Apart from God, the *Kur is* the most precious thing for the Khasi. He/she finds happiness when he/she is loved and valued by his/her *Kur.* The worst punishment that he/she is afraid of is to be ostracized from his/her *Kur.* All of the above religious-ethical norms focus on the idea of maintaining right and responsible relationship. For the Khasi, the idea of right relationship connotes justice, equality and liberation in all aspects of life. Therefore, all of them have a very close affinity to the concept of *Kamai ia ka Hok.* In order to earn righteousness in his/her life the maintaining of the responsible and just relationship in all aspects of life is very fundamental.

4.4. *Kamai ia ka Hok* (earn righteousness): A Theological-Ethical Paradigm

As stated above, the principle of *Kamai ia ka Hok* has a deep impact on the Khasi society. It advocates justice, equality and liberation in terms of maintaining right and responsible relationship between human-human and God-human dimensions. Therefore, it acts as a paradigm for the theological, ethical and social outlook of the Khasi. In the following lines attempt will be made to construct a viable theological-ethical pattern using the concept of *Kamai ia ka Hok.*

4.4.1. *Kamai ia ka Hok* (earn righteousness): A Norm for Justice and Equality

Kamai ia ka Hok emphasizes on justice and equality. *Ka Hok* or righteousness focuses on right and responsible actions governed by the dictum 'to know human is to know God' *(tip briew tip blei).* Sib Charan Roy comments that in the Khasi understanding justice means focusing on what is right and just in everything one does. He further adds that what the Khasi proclaim is justice to be advocated in all spheres of life.[11] This reflects the fact that to be righteous for a Khasi would mean to practice justice to a fellow human being. This sprang out of the, idea that that God has sent human being into this world to strive for righteousness by being just in all dealings. The Khasi believe that to know God is to do good and act justly in all relationships. Gustavo Gutierrez in his book *The Power of the Poor in History* also affirms this idea. He says, "Knowledge of God is love of God. To Know God means to love God. To know God is to do justice."[12] The emphasis here is on our relationship with God which is expressed in our relationship with our fellow human beings. To be in relationship with God demands the expression of this experience in the promotion of justice on an inter-human level of relationship.[13] Commutative justice- the kind of justice that deals

[11] Sib Charan Roy, *Ka Niam Ki Khasi...*, 10.

[12] Gustavo Gutierrez, *The Power of the Poor in History* (London: SCM Press, 1983), 8.

[13] Leonilla V. Bermisa, "Justice: The Way to Reconciliation and Healing," *God's Image 21/2* (June 2002), 7-16, here 9.

with how individuals relate to each other-should be fitted into the wider pattern established by social justice for society as a whole. It means, above all, working to build a society that is intrinsically just-a society in which the structures are just.'[14] The concept of *Kamai ia ka Hok* precisely talk about striving for right relationship with God and fellow beings-therefore, a dictum for building a just society. This is replicated in all the dealings one does in his/her daily life, which puts 'the other' as the frame of reference for justice to be practiced.

On the other hand, *Kamai ia ka Hok* also focuses on maintaining equality in all aspects of life. *Hok* speaks of justice in all relationships; therefore, a just relationship means a society where all are equal irrespective of all the differences. H.O. Mawrie asserts that the Khasi believed that every individual is bestowed with equal rights and dignity. Hence, tampering the rights and integrity of another person is considered evil before human and above all before God.[15] *Kamai ia ka Hok* or striving for righteousness would amount in building a community of equals in terms of justice. To envisage for such a society where justice reigns would be vague without equality being practiced. Thus, righteousness for the Khasi means maintaining a right relationship where dignity and respect of all humans is looked as a primary objective. This is the image for building a society where equality is the *prima facie* requirement.

4.4.2. *Kamai ia ka Hok* (earn righteousness) and Responsibility-Relationality

The Responsibility model is developed by H. Richard Niebuhr. The model focuses on a web of relationships that individuals have to engage in. Relationship patterns are governed by responsibility towards the other persons and individual's response to any situation should lead to social harmony. H. Richard Niebuhr in this model focuses upon persons who act in response to action upon them.[16]

---

[14] Donal Doff, *Spirituality and Justice* (New York: Orbis Books, 1984), 15.

[15] H.O. Mawrie, *Ka Theology Ka Niam Khasi* 1991, 3rd ed. (Shillong: Tmissilda Soh, 2002), 28-30.

[16] H. Richard Niebuhr, *The Responsible Self An Essay in Christian Moral Philosophy* (New York: Harper and Row Publishers, 1963), 56.

The central question for this model is: To whom and for what am I responsible, in what community of relationship am I to be faithful? To this Niebuhr replies, "Responsibility affirms: God is acting in all actions upon you. So respond to all actions upon you as to respond to his action."[17] This means that our actions should involve us in relating responsively to persons and institutions if society so as to contribute toward building a more enriched and wholistic community. In other words, in our responding we are accountable to all humankind and the sovereign God of all creation.[18]

Correspondingly, *Kamai ia ka Hok* as discussed, focuses its attention on responsible actions persons act in a set of relationship. In order to earn righteousness *(Kamai ia ka Hok)* a person needs to act justly and respectfully in all relationships he/she encounters. These responsible actions towards others are governed by the fact that 'all actions are directed to God'. A just and responsible action to fellow human beings is the requirement to strive for the righteousness that God intends. J. K. Tariang opines that the Khasi in the past uphold the principle *ieit ia lade, burom ia kiwei* (love yourself and respect others), which depicts that the individual have the responsibility not only to one self but responsible actions are directed towards others also.[19] Therefore, *Kamai ia ka Hok* is the standard for the Khasi by which all individuals act responsibly in all their relationships in the society. Thus, it accentuates the norm of responsibility in relationship. Responsibility-Relationality is one of the focal points of the implications of *Kamai ia ka Hok* in the life of the Khasi. Responsible actions in relationship to fellow human and God, forms the core of Khasi indigenous theological-ethical thinking.

---

[17] *Ibid.,* 126.

[18] Hunter P. Mabry, *Christian Ethics: An Introductory Reader* (Delhi: ISPCK, 1987), 21.

[19] J.K. Tariang "Ka Bynta Ka Seng Khasi Ha Ka Jaitbynriew," *Seng Khasi Souvenir: 100 Years Celebration, 1899-1999* (Shillong: Seng Khasi, 1999), 36-43, here 42.

4.4.3. *Kamai ia ka Hok* (earn righteousness): A Way to Liberation

Liberation implies a quality of life that asserts the importance and worth of persons in such a way that they are free from control by more powerful interests, or from anything that enslaves them.[20] The goal of liberation is *a community*, which means a unity of persons around the idea that each person is important enough to be respected and loved by all. Major J. Jones opines that liberation entails the consciousness of the real self[21] this consciousness will reveal that human life is dignified and liberated. In the words of Gutierrez:

> It means, in a deeper sense, to see the becoming of mankind *[sic]* as the process of the emancipation of man *[sic]*. It is to see that man *[sic]* in search of a qualitatively different society in which he *[sic]* will be free from all servitude, in which he *[sic]* will be the artisan of his *[sic]* own destiny.[22]

The Khasi understanding of *Hok* or righteousness actually culminates in justice and equality. Every human is worth and has his/her own integrity and dignity. Therefore *Kamai ia ka Hok* teaches every person to respect the right of others by maintaining a just relationship in all aspects of life. This has a liberating tendency in which human being is liberated from all clutches of injustices and oppressive structures. Since human is free from all forms of injustices and inequalities, it therefore reflects a new society free from all kinds of oppression. *Ka Hok or* righteousness in the Khasi understanding therefore, is a 'reservoir-of-meaning' for the liberation of the exploited and the marginalized section of the society. Furthermore, *Kamai ia ka Hok* would mean that each individual is called to practice justice and in the process, every human is given his/her right to be human in the strict sense of the word. Thus, it is also a process of liberation through humanization where every individual irrespective

---

[20] John M. Swomley Jr. *Liberation Ethics* (New York: The Macmillan Company, 1972), 1-5.

[21] Major J. Jones, *Christian Ethics for Black Theology* (New York: Abingdon Press, 1974), 71.

[22] Gustavo Gutierrez, *A Theology of Liberation* (New York: Orbis Books, 1973), 91.

of differences is seen as equal and dignified in the eyes of God, hence, liberated. In the words of Paulo Freire, "liberation is thus childbirth, and a painful one. The man *[sic]* who emerges is a new man *[sic]*, viable only as the oppressor - oppressed contradiction is superseded by the humanization of all men *[sic]*."[23] Liberation thus, incorporates the method of humanization as its very core.

Therefore, it can be argued that *Kamai ia ka Hok* is a way to liberation-as it conscientizes and empowers human to be human. It is actually a vision of a free and liberated society of human being and the whole cosmos.

4.5. *Kamai ia ka Hok* (earn righteousness) vis-a-vis Domestic Violence

As pointed out, *Kamai ia ka Hok is* a viable theological-ethical model in the Khasi indigenous understanding. It has shaped the social, ethical and theological thinking of the Khasi. It incorporates in its corpus the notions of justice, right relationship and liberation. These, therefore, act as a response to any unjust and oppressive structures in the society or family. On the other hand, domestic violence is one of the issues that have marred the present Khasi society in many ways. Violence is an outcome of unjust, bias and oppressive forms of relationship. Therefore, domestic violence connotes a situation of injustice, inequality and oppression. It also means a condition where the notion of power is employed by the powerful to silent and dominate the powerless. In such a situation how can *Kamai ia ka Hok* as an overarching theological-ethical concept be used and applied as a response to the problem of domestic violence in the Khasi matrilineal society? Hence, this section attempts to arrive at a feasible answer to the above question.

4.5.1. *Kamai ia ka Hok* (earn righteousness) as a Tool against Patriarchy: Re-Interpreting Power

The study concentrates on domestic violence between the marital partners, i.e., husband and wife relationship. Therefore, the focus

---

[23] Paulo Freire, *Pedagogy of the Oppressed* (New York: Herder and Herder, 1972), 33.

is on violence that occurs in the context of the family in general and spousal violence in particular. The research also exposes that women are the main targets of domestic violence in the Khasi matrilineal society. Men are also to some extent being victimized in their family. Nevertheless, the extent and intensity of violence differs, and overwhelmingly, majority of the victims are women. Domestic violence as seen in the investigation is an outcome of some ideological factors that operate in the family to oppress and control the dignity of a person. These ideological factors are patriarchy and the use of abusive power.

The study reveals the fact that patriarchy and power function side by side to perpetuate domestic violence (table nos. F.V. and F.VI. Chapter Three) against women in the Khasi matrilineal society. Power in terms of domination is used as an instrument to suppress and silent women in the family through violence. The use of abusive power to control and oppress women in the family by men is a psychological consequence of the society's socialization of men and women. Howard Clinebell argues:

> Men are trained to feel strong and successful only if they are in positions of power. Since power is defined hierarchically, only a few-those on top-can really be powerful. Therefore, most men live with some feeling of failures, powerlessness, and rage. The targets at whom men are conditioned to vent this frustration and rage are those who are weaker and who are socially defined as less significant and powerful. In other words, violence against women is a consequence of the unequal distribution of social status and of economic, political, and legal power between men and women. It is also the consequence of the learned powerlessness and passivity that many women feel when they relate to men.[24]

Therefore, the use of power in controlling women through violence is not just ideological but psychological too. Patriarchy acts

[24] Howard Clinebell, *Basic Types of Pastoral Care and Counselling* (Nashville: Abingdon Press, 1984), 305-306).

as a framework through which such kind of abusive and controlling power is used. Furthermore, patriarchy as a hegemonic power does not provide room for justice and equality to be exercised. Therefore, such a bias understanding has to be confronted.

Kamai ia ka Hok challenges the above distorted understanding of power. It ushers in a new perspective of power and power relations in terms of a right and equal relationship. It emphasizes on justice and equality in all relationships. This includes the relationship between husband and wife in the family. As said earlier, domestic violence occur owing to the misuse of power and the unequal distribution of power and privileges. There is a need therefore, to re-interpret power in a relational aspect. Power should be relational, to build a peaceful and violence-free family. This is precisely what *Kamai ia ka Hok* advocates. It underlines the necessity of a relational power that exists to fabricate existing relationship in the society. The Khasi understand this as the basis of their relationship to one another and God. Speaking on this James Newton Poling opines:

> Power is often misunderstood as a one-way effect on others. But power is actually organized by the relational webs of which we are a part. Our ability to act in effective ways depends on our connections with other power is relational, i.e. the relative amount of power we have is determined in relation to other persons. This gives the person the potential ability to participate fully in relational web ...and to have such an effect on self and others that the whole relational aspect of life is enhanced and enlarged.[25]

Therefore, the use of power in the marital relationship should not be oppressive and dominating. This become abusive and does not give space to a person to express his/her rights. On the other hand relational power as understood in the concept *Kamai ia ka Hok* gives space for freedom and therefore `enhances life'. Relational power also means shared power. Boesak argues, "To share power and

---

[25] James Newton Poling, *The Abuse of Power: A Theological Problem* (Nashville: Abingdon Press, 1991), 24-25).

to share in power is to be fully human. It means to be able to be, to live in accordance with God's given humanity. It means to be able to realize this essential humanity in the socio-historical world in which people have responsibility. Human responsibility presupposes freedom, which is power shared."[26] This means that power is used as a responsibility in relationship to the other person. Such a notion of power builds relationship in the society and does not encourage injustice and inequality. Power here is not oppressive and dominating but enhancing and liberating. The Khasi understanding of *Hok* or righteousness stress this understanding of relational and shared power.

In the context of domestic violence in the Khasi matrilineal society, power through patriarchy is employed to violate and suppress the dignity of women. This has to be confronted. The understanding of power in relational aspect as advocated by *Kamai ia ka Hok is* a tool that challenge patriarchy and the allusive form of power. The above reinterpretation of power is therefore, the response for the misuse and abuse of power by men in the Khasi society in general and family in particular. This ultimately ushers in a new understanding *of* relationship in terms *of Hok* or righteousness-the new power *of* relationship. This new power creates possibilities for the realization *of* full humanity which finds its ideal form in serving justice.

4.5.2. *Kamai ia ka Hok* (earn righteousness): A Model for Right Relationship

The research discloses that most cases *of* domestic violence in the Khasi matrilineal society occur because *of* disturbed relationships. There is a wrong understanding of relationship which results in violence. Factors like alcoholism and extra-marital affairs (table no., F.I. Chapter Three) reflect a distorted relationship between the marital partners. This ultimately leads to serious complications like divorce and suicide, where women are the main victims (table no., G.I. Chapter Three). This eventually affects the relationship with children and their future (table no., G.II. Chapter Three). The

[26] Allan Aubrey Boesak, *Black Theology, Black Power* (Oxford: Mowbray, 1976), 51.

bottom line is therefore, an altered relationship between husband and wife which has to be set right.

Kamai ia ka Hok is a pivotal apparatus through which right relationship can be understood meaningfully in the society in general and family in particular. The Khasi believe that maintaining right or just relationship with all human beings is an essential criterion to understand God. Relationship with God is measured through relationship with others. A Khasi is thus, expected to strive for righteousness through right or just relationship with other people. *Kamai ia ka Hok* therefore, operates as a theological ethical paradigm for understanding right relationship in the context of domestic violence.

Domestic violence implies a situation of oppression, domination and subjugation of one of the marital partners by the other. It is an environment where one of the partners is an oppressor (mostly men) and the other an oppressed (mostly women). Freire argues that with the establishment of a relationship of oppression, violence has already begun.[27] So whenever oppression through violence is involved a relationship is defined as unhealthy and disturbed. Freire further evaluates that in such a relationship violence is initiated by the dominant against the subordinate, in his words, "it is not the tyrannized who initiate despotism but the tyrants."[28] Such a relationship can be rectified through a just or right view of relationship. *Kamai ia ka Hok* speaks of right relationship in terms of justice, so right relationship is nothing but the practice of justice in a given relationship. In a situation of domestic violence it would mean a right or just relationship between the partners in a marital relationship.

Right relationship is the outcome of responsible action which is directed towards the other. This relationship for Richard Niebuhr is the responsible actions which is a response to God's action.[29] Responsible actions therefore, lead to a right or just relationship.

---

[27] Paulo Freire, *Pedagogy of the Oppressed...*, 41.

[28] *Ibid.*, 41.

[29] FL Richard Niebuhr, *The Responsible Self...*, 126.

According to Joseph Fletcher, this just or right relationship is maintained through one criterion called 'love'. In his words:

> Situation ethics has only one norm or principle or law that is binding and exceptionable, always good and right regardless of the circumstances. That is love-the *agape* of the summary commandment to love God and the neighbor.[30]

Therefore, justice in a marital relationship means that love should bind the partners together. *Kamai ia ka Hok* explicates the idea of respecting each other in a relationship by honoring the dignity and integrity of a person. Every Khasi is called upon to earn righteousness by respecting the other person. This in other words, would mean 'love of a neighbor' in a Christian understanding. Fletcher thus asserts, "Love is justice or that justice loves. They are one and the same. To be loving is to be just, to be just is to be loving."[31] Hence, love is a criterion for right relationship. The Khasi understanding of *Hok* elucidates the idea of a right or just relationship maintained through justice which has its base on love. In other words, *Hok* or righteousness means love in practice. Boesak opines that love is always love in righteousness.[32]

It is in such a context of justice through love that a right relationship can be established. Domestic violence mirrors a disturbed or distorted relationship. This can be set right when justice and love occupies their place in a relationship between husband and wife. Such a relationship based on love can transform the oppressor and the oppressed, the dominant and the subordinate. It is an approach that views a relationship through the lens of justice and love. It brings in a new dimension to humanity because it opposes injustice and oppression and foster humanization and the right to be human in the strict sense of the term. It is therefore, apt to end with the words of Paulo Freire who says:

---

[30] Joseph Fletcher, *Situation Ethics* (Philadelphia: The Westminster Press, 1966), 30.

[31] *Ibid.*, 93.

[32] Boesak, *Black TAdobe Garamond Proheology Black Power...*, 146.

> It is-paradoxical though it may seem- precisely in the response of the oppressed to the violence of their oppressors that a gesture of love may be found. Consciously or unconsciously, the act of rebellion by the oppressed... can initiate love. Whereas the violence of the oppressors prevents the oppressed from being fully human, the response of the latter to this violence is grounded in the desire to pursue the right to be human. As the oppressors dehumanize others and violate their rights, they themselves also dehumanized. As the oppressed, fighting to be human, take away the oppressors' power to dominate and suppress, they restore to the oppressors the humanity they had lost in the exercise of oppression.[33]

4.5.3. *Kamai ia ka Hok* (earn righteousness): Toward an inclusive Community of Equal and Liberated Partners

The study reveals that most cases of domestic violence in the Khasi matrilineal society occur due to inequality. It is very clear that majority of the victims are women (table nos., E.I. and E.11. Chapter Three). This goes on to show that unequal treatment, unequal distribution of power and opportunities in the family and society are the major causes of domestic violence in the Khasi society. As being mentioned earlier, women are treated as inferior in many ways. The Khasi projected men as more powerful than women. The saying that a man is divinely endowed with *Khadar buit khadar bor* (high intellect and strength) and a woman with *shibuit shibor* (low intellect and strength) reflects the fact about how women are treated in the family and society at large. This has a repercussion on the attitude and mentality of men, of which domestic violence against women is one of them. Therefore, we see from the study that the Khasi men exercise patriarchy (table no., F.V. Chapter Three) to dominate and violate the dignity and humanity of women in the domestic set up. These facts go on to show that the Khasi society

[33] Freire, *Pedagogy of the Oppressed...*, 41-42.

does not practice equality and women in many cases are victimized in the process. Thus, a tangible and viable response has to be made in order to envisage a community of equal participation and sharing. *Kamai ia ka Hok is* an over-arching theological-ethical consideration that envisions a world where equality and dignity of a person are its foundations. The Khasi society has used the above concept to determine their relationship with fellow human beings and God. Nevertheless, it is not being implemented when it comes to the relationship of husband and wife in the family. Culture has been used by men to suppress women in the society and family. Therefore, a re-interpretation of the above thought from an ethical perspective pertaining to the relationship in the family is deemed necessary. If equality which leads to actual liberation of humanity in the context of oppression is the catch word of *Kamai ia ka Hok,* it has to be seen first in the family. A right elucidation of relationship based on equality is indeed mandatory, if we are to build a community of equal partners in the family and society.

Kamai ia ka Hok by stressing on maintaining right or just relationship, visualizes a society of equality between men and women. It has to be a relationship based on mutual sharing and respect of each other. In a context of domestic violence, it is a relationship where love and respect replace hatred and violence. This relationship is not to see the other person as an object to be used and manipulated according to the whims and fancies of the powerful. On the contrary, it is a bond of respect to the dignity and integrity of the other person as equal in the eyes of God. Martin Buber, a Jewish Philosopher, speaks of equality in terms of relationships which is based on *I-Thou* not *I- It.* He opines that *I- It* is a relationship where the other person is looked upon as an object. On the other hand, I-*Thou* is a relationship of respect, where the other person is perceived as equals. In his own words:

> Whenever the sentence "I see the tree" is so uttered that it no longer tells of a relation between the man *[sic] - I-* and the *tree-Thou-* , but establishes the perception of the tree as an object by the human consciousness, the barrier

> between subject and object has been set up. The primary *I-It,* the word of separation, has been spoken.[34]

Therefore, a relationship of equality is a relationship where human beings whether male or female are respected and honored. In situation of domestic violence, it is an *I- Thou* relationship where both sexes are projected as equal, not a relationship of *I-It* where one of them is objectified. The relationship is not a subject-object dualism but of equal participation, esteem and dignity. *Kamai ia ka Hok* clearly emphasizes on this very understanding of relationship based on justice and equality of all irrespective of the differences. For the Khasi, if *Kamai ia ka Hok* (to earn righteousness) is the main religious and social-ethical teaching then everybody are called to strive for a just and inclusive society based on equality. Such a society envisages liberation of all human beings from all the clutches of injustices and oppression. Once equal opportunities and equal distribution of power relations are emphasized, we would be no doubt anticipating a violence-free society. This would be indeed identical to envisioning a new heaven or new earth-a new society. In the words of Ruether:

> The center of such a new society would have to be not just the appropriate new social form, but a new social vision, a new soul that would inspire the whole. Society would have to be transfigured by the glimpse of a new type of social personality, a 'new humanity' appropriate to a 'new earth'. One might call this a 'new religion', if one understands by this prophetic vision to shape a new world on earth, and not an alienated spirituality.[35]

In such 'a new society' all are liberated from all oppression and bondages therefore, stand equal and dignified in the eyes of a fellow human and above all in the eyes of God. Domestic violence has disfigured the Khasi society, where men and women are suffering the consequences. It is a time now to call for everyone to *Kamai*

---

[34] Martin Buber, *I and Thou* (New York: Charles Scribner's Sons, 1958), 23.

[35] Rosemary Radford Ruether, *New Woman, New Earth* (New York: The Seabury Press, 1975), 210-211.

ia ka Hok (earn righteousness) in striving and envisioning 'a new society' of equal and liberated people, male and female-as intended by God. This vision involves the working toward such a society by all irrespective of the differences on the basis of gender, class or religion.

4.6. Suggestions: The Road Ahead

The above is an attempt to arrive at a viable theological-ethical response to the problem of domestic violence in the Khasi matrilineal society. *Kamai ia ka Hok* (earn righteousness) is a frame of reference used by the researcher to evolve the criteria for the same. Nevertheless, domestic violence is a concern owing to its intensity with which it affects the fabric and dimension of the Khasi society and family. This section therefore, is an effort to propose the following suggestions to the Khasi society and Church as a vision ahead in attempting to counteract domestic violence:

- *Kamai ia ka Hok* (earn righteousness) and other traditional concepts can act as an interlocutor through which the Khasi culture and Christianity can come together in responding to issues like domestic violence. The Khasi Church has not paid much attention to the traditional values enshrined in the culture as they are looked upon as inferior to the Christian teachings or values. The Church is therefore, called to re-capture and re-interpret those concepts, which are otherwise also being neglected by the present Khasi generation. This will lead into a new understanding of Khasi indigenous theological-ethical thinking in responding to the issues affecting the Khasi ethos. The Church should play a role in conscientizing about righteousness in terms of justice and right relationship in the society and family. Domestic violence is an outcome of unequal and unjust relationship between man and woman in the family. The church is called to use its available ventures to conscientize and sensitize people about this issue and teach them to live a righteous life through maintaining right or just relationship in the family in particular and society in general. The following proposals can be made:

- Pulpit Ministry' or `Preaching' should be the place to teach and exhort people to live a happy family life, in terms of equality and respect of human dignity. Bible studies and other forms of teachings can also serve as means to advocate gender equality and justice through right relationship. Attempts should be made to avoid androcentric language which promotes inequality and patriarchal domination. Instead, a more inclusive use of language in preaching and teaching should be encouraged to build a just and equal community.
- Sunday schools' can be the right platform through which children and adults can be taught about respecting the dignity and integrity of another person in the eyes of God.
- The Church through its women's and youth wings can organize workshops, seminars, awareness programs on domestic violence. The process is to sensitize people about the intensity and dimension of the issue and to teach them to shun violence. Such endeavors should also involve NGOs and governmental agencies. This will serve as tools to inform people about the possible judicial and governmental aids when such situation is encountered in the future.
- The Church should make use of church magazines, periodicals and other writings to criticize domestic violence and advocate just relationship based on equality. This will be another step of conscientizing people about the malady of domestic violence and the process of enhancing relationship patterns in the family and society.
- Special pastoral care and counseling should be made available especially to those affected families. Visitations, teachings, prayers and counseling will definitely help in this regard.
- The Government and NGOs can play a more pro-active role in conscientizing people about the issue. The study exposed that most people are not aware on certain legal procedures concerning domestic violence (table no. I. sub section 3.9. Chapter Three), like the Protection of

Women from Domestic Violence Act, 2005. Awareness of such legal aids is an urgent need if we are to speak of dealing with the issue concretely.

- Media can play a prominent role in sensitizing about gender issues and their related problems. This helps in bringing a consciousness to the masses for building a just and equal society. Print and visual media should act as means through which issues like domestic violence can be dealt effectively. They will also serve as areas where people can be conscientized to build relationship in the society and family based on mutual respect and dignity as advocated by concept like *Kamai ia ka Hok* (earn righteousness).
- Schools and colleges and other places of learning can be agencies where people are made aware of domestic violence and its affect on familial and societal life. They can also operate as places where gender sensitization, gender equality and dignity are emphasized.
- Literatures based on the subject matter should be encouraged. These will serve as devices to bring in awareness and conscientize people about maintaining equality, justice to all irrespective of differences in gender, class and status. The present research deals only with domestic violence concerning spousal or marital relationship. Further researches are called for domestic violence against children, old-aged and domestic workers. In addition, matrilineal system and the transitions that have taken place over the years can be another area for further research.

Conclusion

Kamai ia ka Hok (earn righteousness) is indeed an overarching theological-ethical corpus in the Khasi indigenous understanding. We have noted that this concept is employed as a response to domestic violence in the Khasi matrilineal society. *Kamai ia ka Hok* focuses on justice, equality and liberation, which are the criteria of building a violence-free society or family. The crux of the matter is that we can never achieve such a condition without establishing right or just relationship among human beings or between husband and wife in the context of a family. The Khasi believe that this can be attained when each human aspire for *Ka Hok* or righteousness. We have therefore, seen that the above concept is deemed appropriate in situation of domestic violence. It visualizes a society where everybody exercises justice and equality, thus, liberated. This can be done through the maintaining of right relationship in the family and society at large and this specifically is what *Kamai ia ka Hok* envisages. Nevertheless, this is a challenge to the church, society and everybody irrespective of all the differences to strive in building a community of love and respect. This is the vision of a`new humanity' created in and for the image of God-the source of *Ka Hok* or righteousness.

CONCLUSION

The Khasi society practices matrilineal system, in which descend and lineage is traced from the women's side. The overview of the social, cultural, political, economic and religious aspects of the Khasi society reveals that it is a well-established society. Nevertheless, over the years it has undergone tremendous changes brought about by agents like British colonialism, Christianity and of late Globalization. An in-depth examination of the different dimensions of the Khasi society exposes that though women are thought to enjoy better status and position in the society, the actuality is not so. It is seen that patriarchy as a male androcentric and chauvinistic ideology has kept women silent in many ways. This has a repercussion on the family where male power is exhibited through violence. Thus, domestic violence especially against women is the outcome of such a bias male-centered ideology in the Khasi matrilineal society. The other thing discovered is that most of the norms, principles and teachings of the past are neglected today. Most of these values speak volume about maintaining right or just relationship in the society. Therefore, domestic violence is the outcome of a moribund relationship in the society and predominantly family.

Domestic violence has affected many societies across the globe, crossing the barriers of caste, class, status, or even gender. The situation in India is alarming. The study discloses that many women are battered or even killed in their homes. Therefore homes are not the safer places for women. Women suffer different forms/types of domestic violence ranging from physical, emotional, verbal, sexual, psychological, and economical violence. Factors like the situational, cultural, psychological, and religious along with patriarchy and power differentials operate to aggravate domestic violence against women. Different legal mechanisms are endorsed to deal with this dilemma, yet the number of cases rising everyday show that domestic violence is a malady in the Indian society.

It is understood that the major part of the Indian society is patriarchal in nature, so, domestic violence against women is a common phenomenon. Nevertheless, the analysis of data collected proves that domestic violence is a reality in the matrilineal society also. The Khasi matrilineal society is facing domestic violence. The research exposes that most of the victims suffering violence in their homes are women. However, men are also victimized in certain ways. But, the amount and form of violence experienced by women is much more in comparison to men. Therefore, domestic violence against women is a matter of concern. The author opines that domestic violence against women in the Khasi matrilineal society is because of deep-seated factors like patriarchy and power differentials between male and female. This is reflected in the society and particularly in the family. The victimization of women in the family through the use of violence divulges the fact that they are being controlled and oppressed. It was found that patriarchy and the use of male power in the family are the main factors perpetrating domestic violence against women in the Khasi society. Other factors discovered are alcoholism, extra-marital affairs and poverty/unemployment. Furthermore, most women suffer physical, verbal, emotional and sexual forms of domestic violence. On the other hand men suffer only verbal form of violence, but, most of these cases are not exposed owing to the fear of losing one's status and position. The research also reveals that the Government, NGO's and the Church have not done enough to counteract this problem. Nonetheless, the print and visual media are playing a pro-active role in conscientizing and informing the people about this issue. But, this is not enough owing to the fact that in most cases domestic violence is still a hidden matter in the Khasi society. It has to be concretely dealt upon and a viable response has to be made which would serve as a device to counteract this malady that has disfigured the Khasi society.

The researcher is proposing for an indigenous theological-ethical response. For this, the Khasi concept *Kamai Ia ka Hok* (earn righteousness) is employed as a theological-ethical frame to evolve criteria in order to create a feasible response. The author by proposing this, expect to conscientize the Khasi society and church in particular to re-capture this concept which is being ignored by the present Khasi generation. This will therefore, serve as an interlocutor between Christianity and culture. It was found that the above concept stresses on maintaining right or just relationship in the society. This ought to be started from the family which is the basic unit of the society. *Kamai ia ka Hok* focuses on justice, equality and liberation. Therefore, the researcher employed these criteria to confront domestic violence. The argument is that, these criteria evolved, would usher into a new understanding of relationship. This offer as a challenge to the notions of patriarchy and the misuse or abuse of power and act as a paradigm for rectifying distorted relationship in the family. This ultimately ushers in a community of equal and liberated partners, male and female as intended by God-the creator. Therefore, it is a challenge to the Khasi Church and society to realize and re-interpret the importance of the concept *Kamai ia ka Hok,* as a vital theological-ethical tool to counteract domestic violence in the Khasi matrilineal society.

QUESTIONAIRE

Personal Information

Age: ....

Gender: ....

Occupation: ....

Qualification: ....

Marital Status: ....

Address: ....

1. Are you aware of domestic violence?
   (a) Yes b) No
2. If Yes how?
   (a) Through News papers
   (b) Through Television
   (c) In the School/College
   (d) In the Church (e) Anywhere else (specify).
   ....
   ....
3. Are there any cases of domestic violence in your area/locality?
   (a) Yes (b) No
4. When do you think domestic violence started in your area?
   (a) Before the 90's (b) After the 90's
5. Do you agree that women are the main target of domestic violence in your area?
   (a) Yes (b) No

6. If yes, substantiate why and how women are targeted?

   ....

   ....

7. Which type of domestic violence women suffer most in your area? (You can choose more than one answer if needed)
   (a) Physical (b) Verbal (c) Sexual (d) Emotional (e) any other (specify)

   ....

8. On the basis of your choice(s) from the above, substantiate your answer by giving reasons.

   ....

   ....

9. How do you know about the cases of domestic violence? (You can tick more than one reason(s) if needed)
   (a) Cases are reported to the village durbar.
   (b) Cases are reported to the Police.
   (c) Through the role of Media.
   (d) Through the role of various NGO's.
   (e) Any other source. (Specify)

   ....

   ....

10. Do you agree that cases of domestic violence are well reported to the Police?
    (a) Yes (b) No

11. If No, what do you think are the reasons?
    (a) It is taken as a personal matter
    (b) it brings dishonor to the family
    (c) any other reason (specify)

    ....

    ....

12. Does your local Durbar plays an active role when cases of domestic violence are reported?
    (a) Yes (b) No

13. If No, what can be the reasons?
    (a) It is not needed because it is taken as a personal matter
    (b) there is no sufficient law enacted
    (c) It is the matter of police or law
    (d) Any other reasons (specify).

    ....

    ....

14. Are there any sufficient steps taken by the local Durbar to counter act domestic violence in your area?
    (a) Yes (b) No.

15. If Yes or No, state reasons.

    ....

    ....

16. There are some laws and enactments (legal mechanism) that are created to protect and empower women like the Bill on Domestic Violence, 2005; do you agree that they are sufficient to protect domestic violence against women?
    (a) Yes (b) No

17. If yes, give reasons.

    ....

    ....

18. If No, give your reasons or suggestions.

    ....

    ....

19. Do you consider that local print media and visual media play an important role in reporting cases of domestic violence?
    (a) Yes (b) No

20. If you agree or disagree, give reasons.

    ....

    ....

21. Which of the following factors according to you is/are the main cause(s) of domestic violence in your area? (You can one

choose the following reason(s) giving priority based on your own observation).
(a) Alcoholism (b) Drug Addiction (c) Poverty (d) Misunderstanding (e) Extra-marital affairs (f) Suspicion (g) Inferiority complex (h) Jealousy (i) Economic independence.

22. Clearly state the reason(s) of your choice from the above and suggest some more cause (s) if you have.

    ....

    ....

23. The victims of domestic violence resort to:
    (a) Divorce (b) Suicide (c) any other (Specify)
24. Substantiate your choice by giving reasons.

    ....

    ....

25. On the basis of your choice above, whom do you think will be the worst affected?
    (a) Wife (b) Husband (c) Children
26. State the reasons of your choice from the above.

    ....

    ....

27. Do you agree that men are also victims of domestic violence in the Khasi matrilineal society?
    (a) Yes. (b) No
28. If yes, substantiate your answer by giving reasons.

    ....

    ....

29. Do you agree that Pornography is a factor that perpetuates domestic violence against women in the Khasi society?
    (a) Yes (b) No
30. If yes, which form of violence it leads to?
    (a) Sexual (b) Emotional (c) physical (d) all of the above (e) any other form (Specify) ....

31. If No, give reasons.

    ....

    ....

32. Do you agree that Khasi Matrilineal society is practicing Patriarchal values in many ways?
    (a) Yes (b) No

33. Substantiate your argument by giving reasons.

    ....

    ....

34. Do you think that Power is involved as a controlling mechanism to perpetuate domestic violence?
    (a) Yes (b) No

35. If Yes or No, substantiate by giving reasons for your argument.

    ....

    ....

36. The impact of globalization on the Khasi socio-cultural ethos can be one of the contributing factors towards domestic violence, do you agree?
    (a) Yes (b) No.

37. If yes, what are the possible reasons? (You can choose more than one answer)
    (a) It gives rise to Individualism (b) It erodes the traditional culture (c) It leads to competitive spirit (d) It empowers women and further discriminates men in the matrilineal set up (e) any other reasons (Specify). ....

38. If No, give reasons.

    ....

    ....

39. The shift from Joint Family to Nuclear family system in the present Khasi society could probably be one of the causes of domestic violence, do you agree?
    (a) Yes (b) No.

40. If Yes or No, what do you think are the reasons?

    ....

    ....

41. Do you agree that the government is taking appropriate steps to deal with domestic violence?
    (a) Yes (b) No

42. If you agree what are the possible steps the government has taken?
    (a) The victims are given adequate care in terms of treatment and shelter (b) They are protected by the law against further violence (c) any other steps (specify)

    ....

    ....

43. If No, give reasons or suggestions.

    ....

    ....

44. The NGOs/ Human Rights Organizations are playing more active role in counter acting domestic violence, do you agree?
    (a) Yes (b) No

45. If yes, what are the steps taken in dealing with domestic violence in general and the victims of violence in particular?

    ....

    ....

    ....

46. If No, give suggestions.

47. Does your Church play a role in solving domestic violence?
    (a) Yes (b) No

48. If yes, what are the steps taken? (You can select more than one answer if needed)
    (a) Bible study are conducted on the subject matter (b) Through women' Fellowship, by conducting awareness programs, workshops and other activities to conscientize the women folk

(c) Counseling (d) Sending to the psychiatrist (e) any other steps taken (specify) ....

....

....

49. If No, what do you think are the reasons?
    (a) Domestic violence is new to the church (b) the church should not interfere as it is a personal matter (c) there is no cases of domestic violence known to the church so far (d) Any other reasons (specify).
50. Is there any possibility to stop or counteract domestic violence in the Khasi society?
    (a) Yes (b) No
51. If yes or no, give reasons and suggestions.

    ....

    ....

BIBLIOGRAPHY

Books

Ahuja, Ram. *Violence Against Women.* New Delhi: Rawat Publications, 2003.

Bareh, *H. A Short History of Khasi Literature.* Shillong: Ri Khasi Press, 1970.

_______ *History and Culture of Khasi People.* Guwahati: Spectrum Publication, 1997.

Bareh, Hamlet. *The History and Culture of Khasi People.* Calcutta: Sarumitra Publishing Ltd., 1967.

Bhandari, J.S., ed. *Kinship and Family in the North East.* Delhi: Cosmo Publication, 1996.

Boesak, Allan Aubrey. *Black Theology, Black Power.* Oxford: Mowbray, 1976.

Bristow, John T. *What Paul Really Said About Women.* New York: Harper and Row, 1998.

Buber, Martin. *I and Thou.* New York: Charles Scribner's Sons, 1958.

Cantlie, K. *Notes on Khasi Laws.* Shillong: Ri Khasi Press, 1971.

Chatterji, Shoma A. *Indian Women, from Darkness to Light.* Calcutta: Parumita Publications, 2000.

_______. *The Indian Women's Search for an Identity.* Delhi: Vikas Publishing House, 1989.

Chattopadhyay, S.K., ed. *Tribal Institutions of Meghalaya.* Guwahati: Spectrum Publications, 1985.

Chowdhury, J.N. *The Khasi Canvas: A Cultural and Political History.* Shillong: Jaya Chowdhury, 1978.

Clinebell, Howard. *Basic Types of Pastoral Care and Counseling.* Nashville: Abingdon Press, 1984.

Conway, Helen *L. Domestic Violence and the Church.* Secunderabad: OM Books, 2003. 2009.

Costa, *G. Ka Riti Jong Ka Ri Laiphew Syiem.* Shillong: Don Bosco Publication, 1994.

Doff, Donal. *Spirituality and Justice.* New York: Orbis Books, 1984.

Dutta, P.N. *Impacts of the West on Khasi and Jaintias: A Survey of Political and Economic Change.* Delhi: Cosmo Publications, 1982.

Filkenhor, D, et.al., *The Dark Side of Families.* London: Sage Publications, 1983.

Fletcher, Joseph. *Situation Ethics.* Philadelphia: The Westminster Press, 1966.

Freire, Paulo. *Pedagogy of the Oppressed.* New York: Herder and Herder, 1972.

Ghosh, SobhaVenkatesh. "Contextualizing Domestic Violence: Family, Community, State." in *Behind CloseDoors: Domestic Violence in India.* Edited by Rinki Bhattacharya. New Delhi: Sage Publications, 2004.

Gurdon, P.R.T. *The Khasis.* Delhi: Cosmo Publication, 1975.

Gutierrez, Gustavo. *A Theology of Liberation.* New York: Orbis Books, 1973.

Gutierrez, Gustavo. *The Power of the Poor in History.* London: SCM Press, 1983.

Haralambos, Michael and Robin Heald. *Sociological Themes and Perspective.* Delhi: Oxford University Press.

Johnson, Holly, et.al., *Violence Against Women.* New York: Springer, 2008.

Jones, Major J. *Christian Ethics for Black Theology.* New York: Abingdon Press, 1974.

Ka Jinglamkhmat Kyllum jong ki Lawyers Collective Halor ka Hok jong ki Kynthei Shillong: North East Network, n.d.

Karlekar, Malavika. "Breaking the Silence." In *Writing the Women's Movement: A Reader.* Edited by Mala Khullar. New Delhi: Zubaan, 2005.

Karotemprel, S, ed. *The Catholic Church in North East India, 1890-1990.* Shillong: Vendrame Institute, 1993.

_______, ed. *The Tribes of North East India.* Shillong: Centre for Indigenous Cultures, 1998.

Kharkongor, Iarington. *Ka Dienshonhi.* Shillong: Self, 1968.

Kharshiing, Hipshon Roy. Ed. *Khasi Heritage.* Shillong: Seng Khasi Publications, 1979.

Khongphai, *A. Principle of Khasi Law.* Shillong, n.p. 1974.

Lachance, Lise. *Marital Violence in Canada: A Journalistic Report.* Bombay: Research Centre for Women's Studies, 1994.

Mabry, Hunter P. *Christian Ethics: An Introductory Reader.* Delhi: ISPCK, 1987.

Madhurima, *Violence Against Women.* New Delhi: Gyan Publishing House, 1996.

Mahajan, A. "Instigators of Wife Battering." In *Violence Against Women.* Edited by Sushma Sood. Jaipur: Arihant Publishers, 1990.

Mahendra, Shivraj Kumar. *A Christian Response to Pornography.* Delhi: ISPCK, 2007.

Mawrie, Barnes L. *Introduction to Khasi Ethics.* Shillong: DBCIC Publications, 2005.

Mawrie, H. Onderson. *Ka Pyrkhat U Khasi.* Shillong: Lyngwiar Press, 1994.

Mawrie, H.O. *Ka Theology Ka Niam Khasi* 1991, 3rd Edition. Shillong: Tmissilda Soh, 2002.

Menon, Niveditha and Michael P. Johnson, "Patriarchy and Paternalism in Intimate Partner Violence: A Study of Domestic Violence in Rural India." In *Recent Studies on Indian Women.* Edited by Kamal K. Misra and Janet Huber Lowry. New Delhi: Rawat Publications, 2007.

Nataranjan, Nalini. *The Missionary among the Khasis.* New Delhi: Sterling Publishing Ltd., 1997.

Niebuhr, H. Richard. *The Responsible Self- An Essay in Christian Moral Philosophy.* New York: Harper and Row Publishers, 1963.

Nigam, Shalu. *Understanding Justice Delivery System from Perspective of Women Litigants as Victims of Domestic Violence in India, Specially in the Context of Section 498A, IPC.* New Delhi: Centre for Women's Development Studies, 2005.

Nongbri, Tiplut. *Gender, Matriliny and Entrepreneurship: The Khasi of North-East India.* New Delhi: Zubaan Publication, 2008.

Poling, James Newton. *The Abuse of Power: A Theological Problem.* Nashville: Abingdon Press, 1991.

Rodborne, T. *U Khasi.* Shillong: Ri Khasi Press, 1979.

Roy, Hipshon, ed. *Khasi Heritage: A Collection of Essays.* Shillong: Seng Khasi, 1996.

Roy, Sib Charan. *Ka Niam Ki Khasi, Ka Niam Tip Briew Tip Blei, 1919* Reprint. Shillong: Ri Khasi Press, 2003.

Ruether, Rosemary Radford. *New Woman New Earth.* New York: The Seabury Press, 1975.

Rymbai, R. Tokin. *Ban Pynieng La Ka Rasong bad Kiwei Kiwei de ki Ese.* Shillong: Witibon Hynniewta Rymbai, 1979.

_______." Some Aspects of the Religion of the Khasi-Pnars." In *Khasi Heritage: A Collection of Essays.* Edited by Hipshon Roy. Shillong: Ri Khasi Press, 1996.

Saul, Jennifer Mather, *Feminism: Issues and Arguments.* New York: Oxford University Press, 2003.

Schneider, David M and Kathleen Gough, eds. *Matrilineal Kinship.* California: University of California Press, 1961.

Sen, Somen, ed. *Women in Meghalaya.* Delhi: Daya Publishing House, 1997.

_______. *Social and State Formation in Khasi and Jaintia Hills.* Delhi: B.R. Publishing Corporation, 1985.

Shadap, Namrita Catherine. *The Origin and Early History of the Khasi Synteng People.* Calcutta: Firma KLM Private Ltd., 1981.

Sib Charan Roy, *Ka Niam Tip Briew Tip Blei.* Shillong: Ri Khasi Press, 1919.

Singh, K. Suresh, ed. *Tribal Situation of India.* Shimla: Indian Institute of Advanced Study, 1972.

Singh, Yogendra. *Culture Change in India: Identity and Globalization.* New Delhi: Rawat Publications, 2000.

Sinha, Niroj. "Profile of Marital Violence: Wife Battering." In *Women and Violence.* Edited by Niroj Sinha. Delhi: Vikas Publishing House, 1989.

Snaitang, O.L. *Christianity and Social Change in North-East India.* Shillong: Vendrame Institute, 1999.

Sten, H. W. ed. *Ki Sngi Jong Ngi.* Shillong: Don Bosco Press, 1994.

Ka History ka Ktien Khasi. Shillong: Self, 1980.

Surtees, Rebecca. "Rape and Sexual Transgression in Cambodian Society." In *Violence Against Women in Asian Societies.* Edited by Lenore Manderson and Linda Rae Bennet. London: Routledge Curzon, 2003.

Swomley Jr., John M. *Liberation Ethics.* New York: The Macmillan Company, 1972.

Vindhya, U. "Battered Conjugality: The Psychology of Domestic Violence." In *The Violence of Normal Times.* Edited by Kalpana Kannabiran. New Delhi: Women Unlimited Publication, 2005.

Vir, Dharam and Kamlesh Mahajan. eds. *Contemporary Indian Women.* Vol. 2. Delhi: Rawat Publications, 1996.

Walby, Sylvia. *Theorizing Patriarchy.* Oxford: Blackwell Publishers, 1990.

Waters, Malcolm. *Modern Sociological Theory.* New Delhi: Sage Publications, 1998.

Journals and Periodicals

Astige, Shanta B. "The Protection of Women from Domestic Violence Act, 2005: Its relevance to the present Indian society." *Legal News and Views* 21/10 (October 2007): 11-14.

Bermisa, Leonilla V. "Justice: The Way to Reconciliation and Healing." *God's Image* 21/2 (June 2002): 7-16.

Dobash, R.E. and R.P. Dobash, "Wives: The Appropriate Victims of Domestic Violence." *Victimology* 2/314 (March-June 1978): 430-454.

"Domestic Violence Rises in India." *Legal News and Views 21/4* (April 2007): 13-14. Durrany, Seema. "Legal Responses to Domestic Violence in India." *Legal News and Views* 19/10 (November 2005): 4-6.

Kurian, Jessy. "Some Aspects of the Protection of Women from Domestic Violence Act, 2005." *Legal News and Views 22/1* (January-June 2008): 7-8.

Kurian, Jose. "Protection of Women from Domestic Violence." *Legal News and Views* 20/1 (January 2006): 8-9.

Nigam, Shalu. "Law on Domestic Violence: An Urgent Need to Break Silence." *Legal News and Views* 20/12 (December 2006): 4-5.

Nongbri, Tiplut. "Gender and the Khasi Family Structure, Some Implications of the Meghalaya Succession to Self-Acquired Property Act 1984." *The Sociological Bulletin* 37/122 (March-September 1998): 75-82.

Reddy, Shiela. "Domestic Violence." *Women's Link 7/1* (January-March 2001): 3-5. Tariang, J.K. "Kamai ia ka Hok." *Sneng Khasi* 73/10 (November 1997): 15-21.

Scaria, Mary. "Domestic Violence Act: Will Women be safe Now?." *Legal News and Views* 19/10 (December 2005): 4-6.

Souvenir

Rymbai R.T. "U HynniewTrep bad la kaNiam." *Seng Khasi Souvenir.* Shillong: Seng Khasi, 1986.

Synrem, Kelian. "Religion of the Khasis." *Seng Khasi Souvenir: 100 Years Celebration, 1899-1999.* Shillong: Seng Khasi, 1999.

Tariang, J.K. "Ka Bynta Ka Seng Khasi Ha Ka Jaitbynriew." *Seng Khasi Souvenir: 100 Years Celebration, 1899-1999.* Shillong: Seng Khasi, 1999.

Newspapers

The Shillong Times (Shillong), 20 August 2004.

The Shillong Times (Shillong), 28 November 2008.

Unpublished Materials

Dohling, Barbara. "Interrogating the Importance and Significance of *Tip Briew Tip Blei* (to know People is to know God) for developing an Ethical Critique of the Contemporary Khasi Society." Unpublished M.Th. Thesis, Senate of Serampore, 2008.

Kharlukhi, B.R. "Syiemship in the Khasi Hills Up to 1858 AD." Unpublished Ph.D. Thesis, Guwahati University, 1980.

Khongwir, W.C. "A Christian Ethical Response to Ecological Problems in the Khasi Hills of Meghalaya." Unpublished M.Th. Thesis, Senate of Serampore College, 1987.

Lyngdoh, B.C. "The Concept of God in the Khasi Tradition and its Implications for Christianity." Unpublished B.D. Thesis, Senate of Serampore College, 1976.

Dictionaries and Encyclopedia

Brown, Lesley ed. *The New Shorter Oxford English Dictionary.* Vol. l. Oxford: Clarendon Press, 1993.

Davidson, G.W. M.A. Seaton and J. Simpson, eds., *Chambers Concise 20th Century Dictionary.* New Delhi: Allied Publishers Ltd., 1991.

Gurdon P.R.T., "Khasis," *Encyclopedia of Religion and Ethics.* Edited by James Hastings. Vol. 7 (New York: Charles Scribner's Sons Publication, 1955): 690-692.

Piepmeier, Alison. "Domestic Violence." In *The Women's Movement Today: An Encyclopedia of Third Wave Feminism.* Edited by Leslie L. Heywood. Vol. 1 (New Delhi: Rawat Publications, 2005): 96-97.

Strauss, A. "Wife Beating (1629-1934)," *Encyclopedia of Crime and Justice,* edited by Sanforn H. Karkirl (New York: Free Press, 1983): 1-10.

Internet Material

"Shillong." http://en.wikipedia.org/wiki/shillong (28 Jan 2010).

National Family Health survey 2015-2016, http://www.meghalaya.pdf.rchilps.org>nfhs. Accessed March 6, 2019.

National Family Health survey 2015-2016, http://www.oxfamindia.org>2018. Accessed March 6, 2019.

http://www.megpolice.gov.in>crime_statistics.html. Accessed 6 March 2019.

"Matrilineal Society also tops in Domestic Violence", http://wwww.shillongtimes.com, December 16 2014, accessed on October 16 2018.

Interviews

Diengdoh, Sweetie. Retired Government Servant, Shillong. Interview, 29 May, 2009.

Dkhar, I. Medical Report Technician, Civil Hospital Shillong. Interview, 14 September, 2012.

Kharlukhi, B.R. Church Elder, Shillong. Interview, 16 September, 2009.

Laloo, B. Headman Lawjynriew Shillong. Interview, 12 September, 2009.

Lamar, Rica. Vice Chairperson, Meghalaya State Women Commission. Interview, 16 September, 2009.

Lyngwa, I.D. The District Social Welfare Officer, Shillong. Interview, 2 May, 2009.

Mawlong, D.S. Headman, Kenches Trace, Oxford and Rilbong, Shillong. Interview, 12 September, 2009.

Mukhim, Patricia. Padmashree Awardee, Shillong. Interview, 9 January, 2012.

Phanbuh, Theilin. Social Worker, Shillong. Interview, 2 June 2009.

Phanbuh, Theilin. Chairperson Meghalaya State Commission for Women. Interview, 6 March, 2019.

Prasad, K. Officer in Charge, Sadar Police Station, Shillong. Interview, 15 September, 2009.

Sohtun, Annie. Social Worker, North East Network, Shillong. Interview, 26 May, 2009.